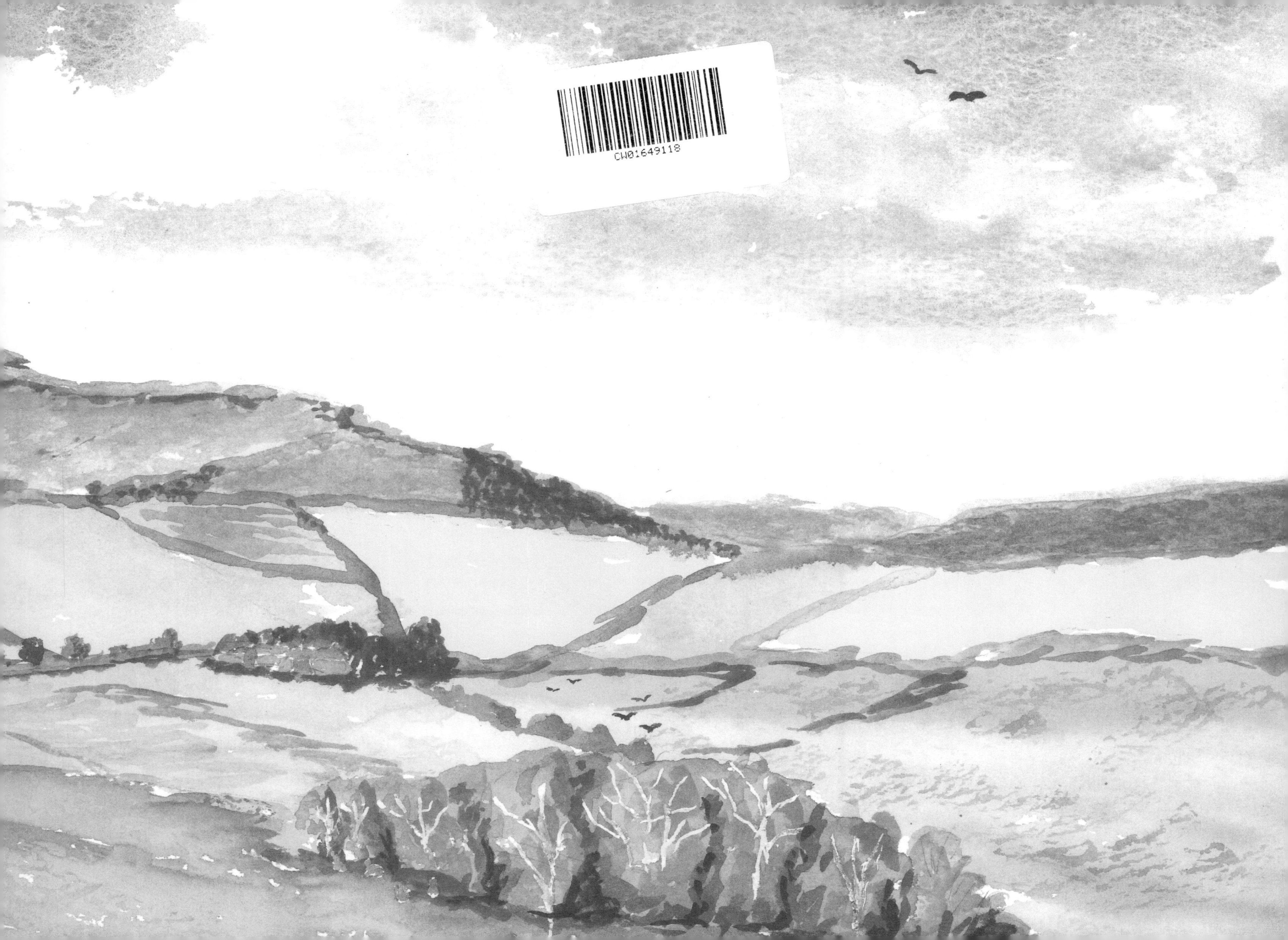

To Keith

Many Thanks

Bob Gilhooley

& Brian

The Picturesque Cotswolds

A Souvenir In Beautiful Paintings

By Artist Bob Gilhooley

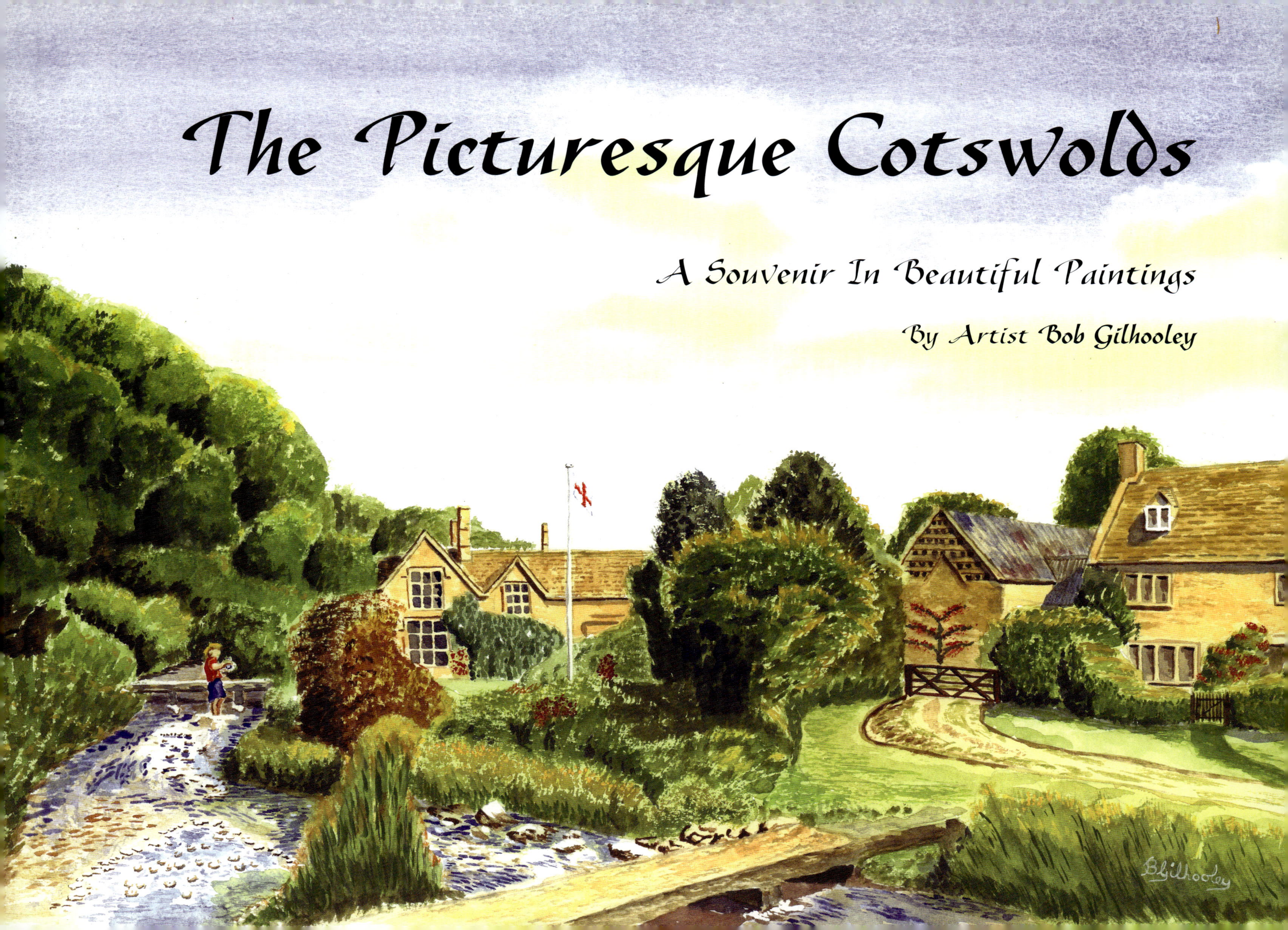

The Picturesque Cotswolds

A Souvenir In Beautiful Paintings

By Artist Bob Gilhooley

Published By

Reardon Publishing

PO Box 919 Cheltenham GL50 9AN

Tel: 01242 231800 Email: Reardon@bigfoot.com

Website: www.reardon.co.uk

ISBN (13) 9781874192039

Front Cover picture: Upper Slaughter

End Papers, front & back : The Wolds

Inside Intro: Towards Stanton

Artist Bob Gilhooley

Email bobgilhooley@aol.co.uk

Printed in China through World Print Ltd

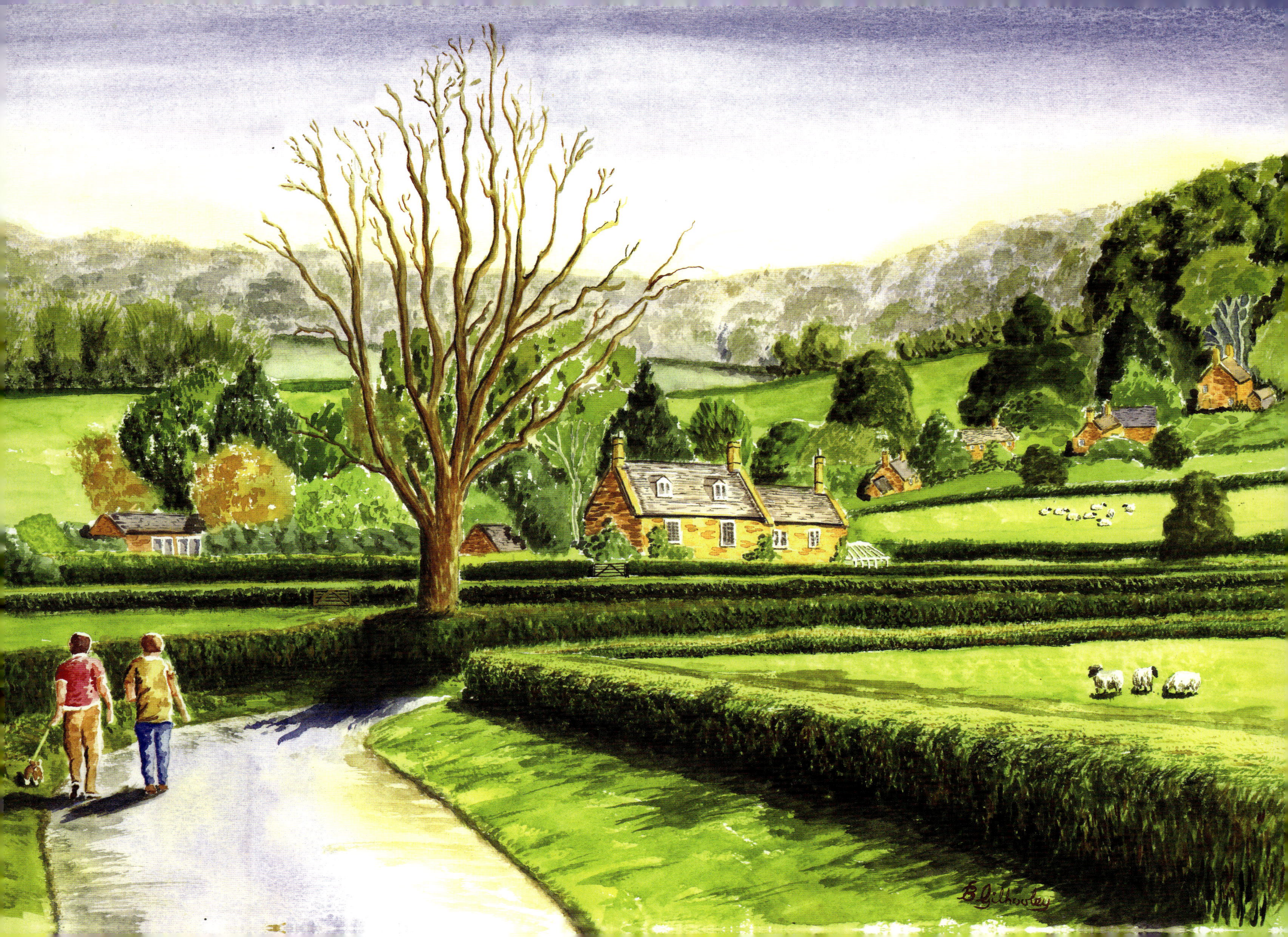
B.Githowley

Contents

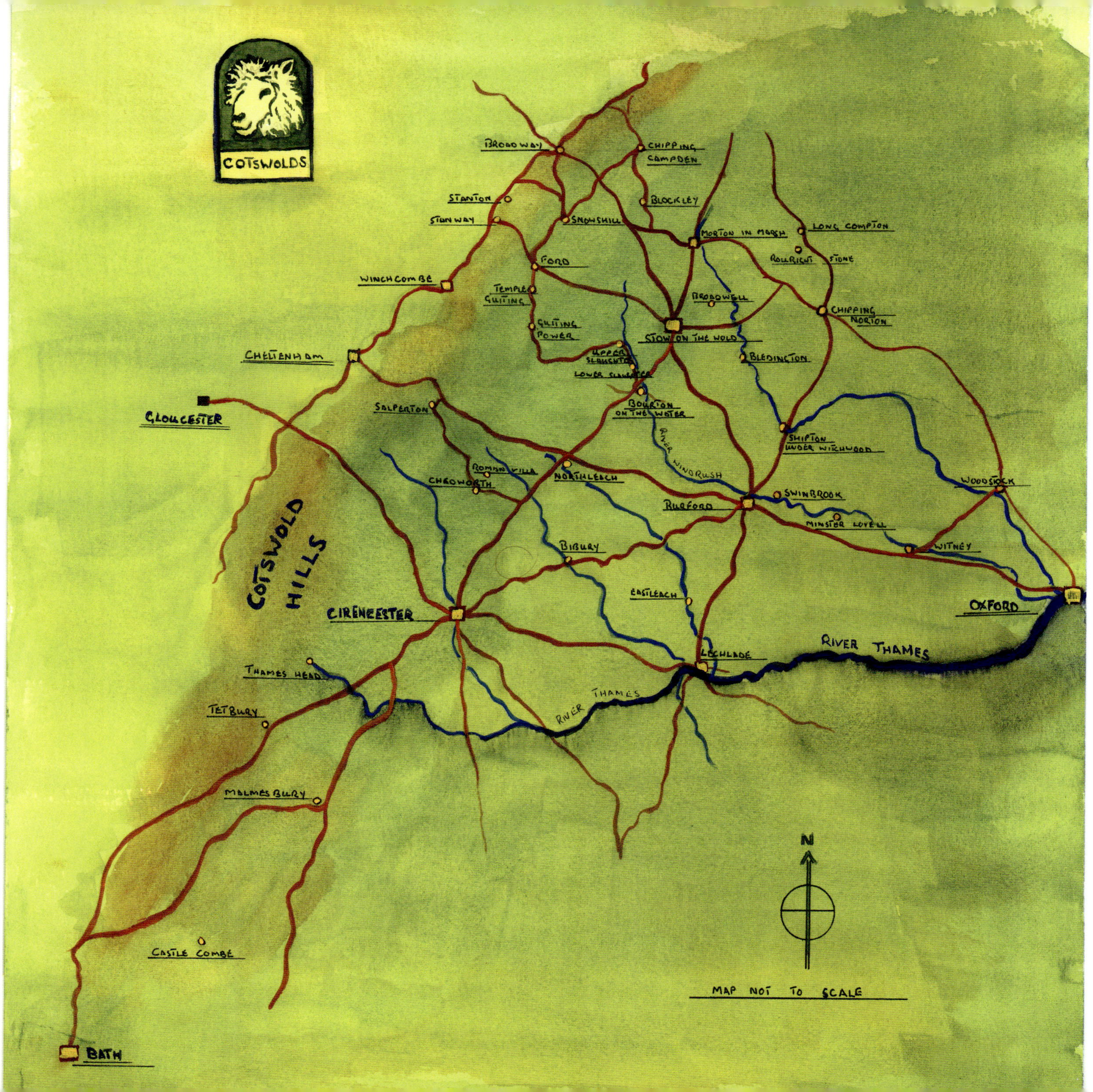

COTSWOLDS
BROADWAY
CHIPPING CAMPDEN
STANTON
STANWAY
SNOWSHILL
BLOCKLEY
MORTON IN MARSH
LONG COMPTON
ROLLRIGHT STONE
FORD
WINCHCOMBE
TEMPLE GUITING
BROADWELL
CHIPPING NORTON
GUITING POWER
STOW ON THE WOLD
UPPER SLAUGHTER
LOWER SLAUGHTER
BLEDINGTON
CHELTENHAM
GLOUCESTER
SALPERTON
BOURTON ON THE WATER
RIVER WINDRUSH
SHIPTON UNDER WITCHWOOD
ROMAN VILLA
CHEDWORTH
NORTHLEACH
SWINBROOK
WOODSTOCK
BURFORD
MINSTER LOVELL
WITNEY
BIBURY
COTSWOLD HILLS
EASTLEACH
OXFORD
CIRENCESTER
LECHLADE
RIVER THAMES
THAMES HEAD
RIVER THAMES
TETBURY
MALMESBURY
CASTLE COMBE
BATH
N
MAP NOT TO SCALE

Meandering through the Cotswolds

Preamble

Visitors to this part of the country probably think " What a lovely day to drive through the countryside."
And you are right! It is a lovely part of England to drive around.
But please don't just drive through. Get out of your tin box on wheels and have a look around.
Think of the delights of staying in an 18th century Coach House Inn. Then after a traditional breakfast.
Take a walk around the town or village you have chosen to stay in. Not just the High Street,
but go up the side street and lanes. Say Hello to the man tending his garden.
Say good morning to the lady walking her dog. Walk into the open countryside.
Lean against an old dry stone wall or five bar gate and "Look at the day !"
Smell the fresh air with possibly a gentle breeze on your face.
Hear the Cotswolds talking to you! With a Caa Caa of the Rooks over in the spinney.
The Baah of the sheep's bleating in that field over there or the cough–call of a Pheasant.
The tinkle and gurgle of a stream a few feet away. Trickling down to the hollow.
And see over the next Wold. A village with the early morning sun stroking one side
of the old church tower. and beckoning to you.
Yes the area you are in is beautiful. Designated an Area Of Outstanding Beauty.
Let me share some of it with you in Sympathetic Watercolour Paintings
We start in the North near to Stratford on Avon.

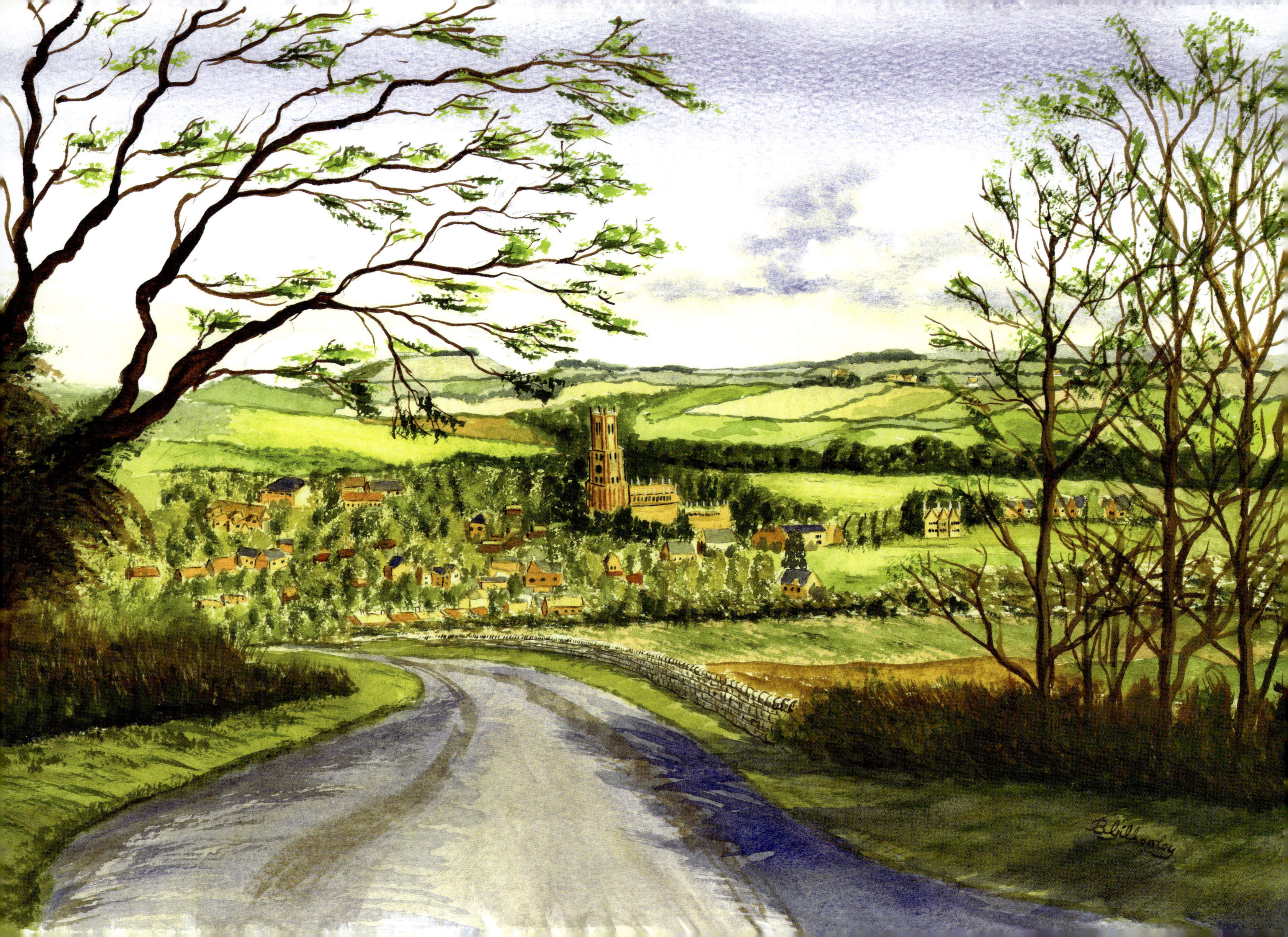
B Gilhooley

Moreton - In - Marsh

We head into the North Cotswolds along the Fosse Way. A major roman road from Leicester to Cirencester.
Moreton, is a true Cotswold town in beautiful mellow golden stone.
A market was granted by the King probably around the early 1200s
Over the early years the prosperity of the town grew and waned frequently,
until the late 17th early 18th century
The then Lord Redesdale who became Lord of the Manor and great benefactor
to the area reinstated the market on land to the west side of the Fosse Way.
It was he who built Redesdale Hall. The Town Hall on the main street.
With the increase in horse drawn coach traffic London-Birmingham and the West.
London-Coventry to the North. Moreton became a major coaching halt.
Many Coaching Inns with stabling grew in the 1800s. Some hostelries still exist today.
One retaining the name. The Redesdale Arms. And very good it is too.
The buildings either side of the market place are many and varied in interest.
The 16th Century Curfew Tower and Bell still remain. It was rung nightly in the Middle ages
to encourage the good people of the town to return home. For work awaits them in the morn.
And to remind residents to extinguish candles etc. for the great fear of fire due to thatch roofs.
Many small independent shops and antique shops continue to prosper here today.
Morton Show is held September every year. A country show one should not miss.

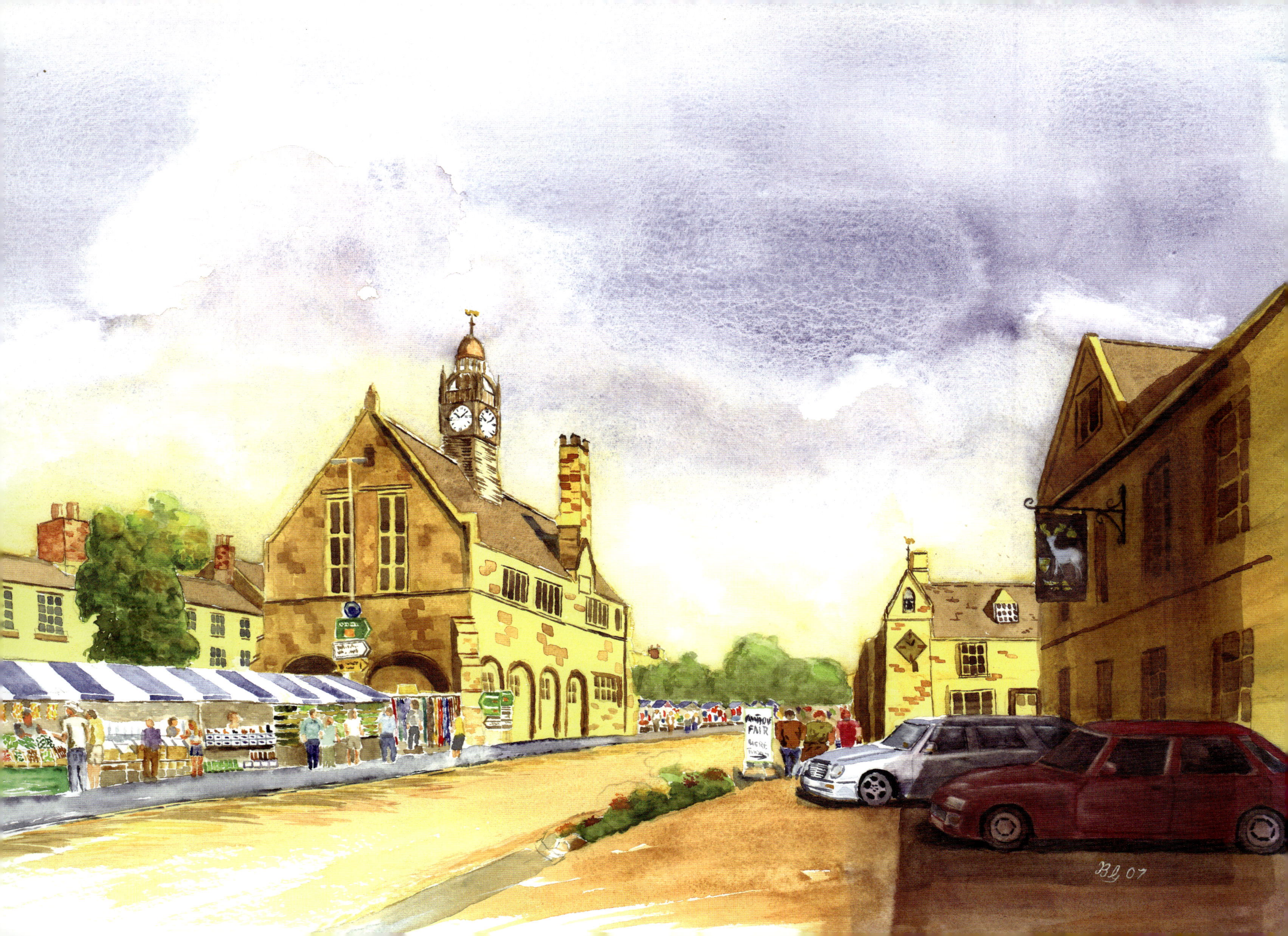
FAIR

Blockley

This is one of my favourite Villages. Set in a steep valley .
The cottages, 2 & 3 storey houses and numerous Mills cling tightly to the hillsides.
To get a feel of the village . I suggest you park on the main road as you come in.
Spend a couple of hours then, walking around Blockley.
Head towards the imposing Church. You will pass the recreation park with its Bowls Club.
The village shop and cafe is run by a cooperative of the villagers
Walk along the High Street which narrows to a single car width.
You can walk along to the footpath taking you to the fish ponds
"Why was a Fish celibrated on its death ? And where ?"
Narrow lanes lead off Left and right.
These all have little secrets for you to discover and if you like photography.
Every turn looking across the valley gives you a new vista.
Turning down into the bottom of the valley you will come across the fast flowing stream
which was the life blood of the village. It was the power for the numerous Wool and later
Silk Mills in the village. Visit Mill Dean where the gardens are open to the public.
The stream flows through many gardens and across the front of one cottage.
After your walk, there are two good hostelries in the village.
The Crown Hotel boasts a superb menu. Also The Great Western Pub will give you a very adequate fill.

From Blockley we travel to Chipping Campden.

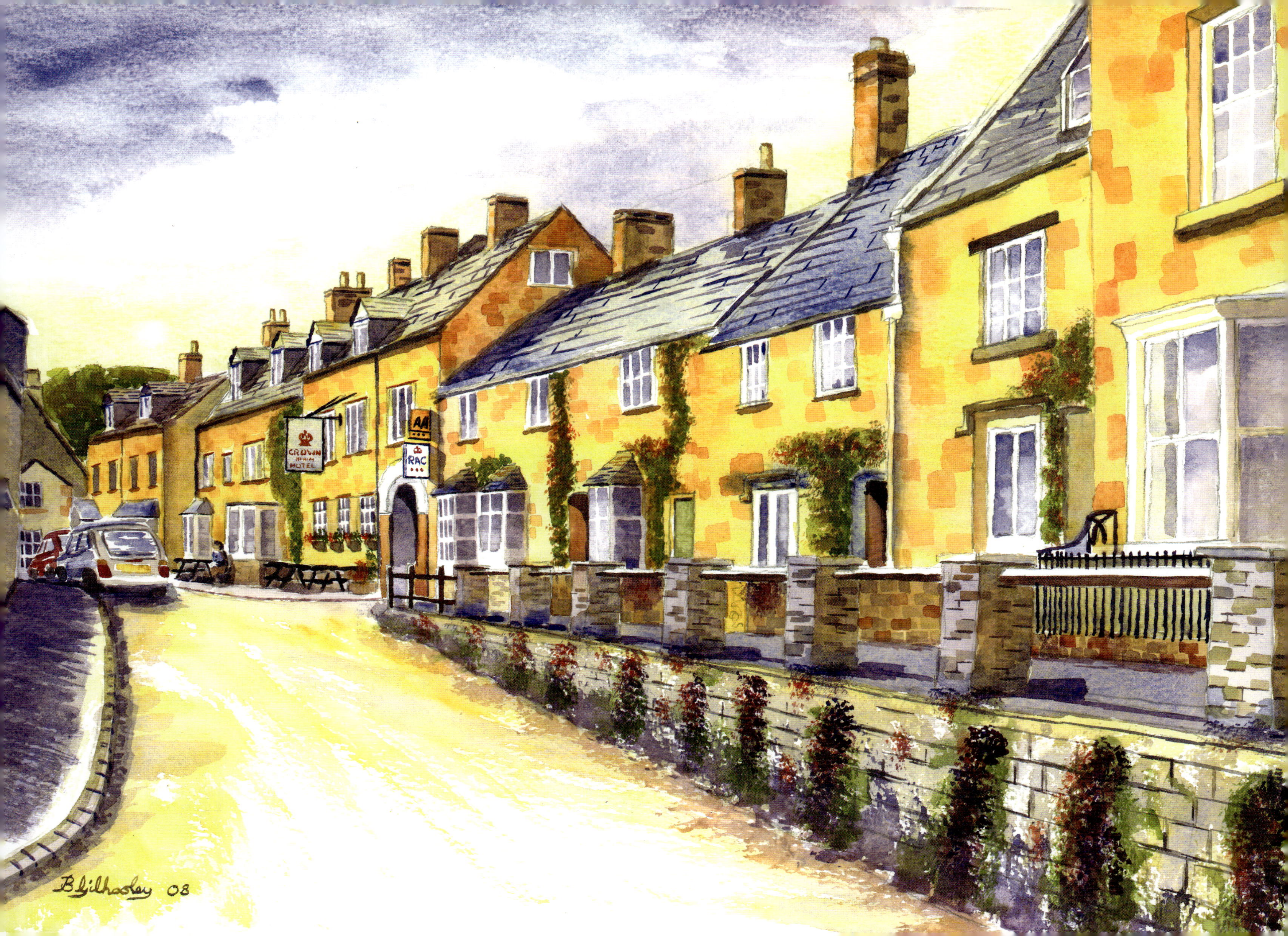
CROWN
HOTEL
AA
RAC
08

Chipping Campden

Another Gem. Chipping Campden and Broad Campden are most pretty.
Broad Campden has one of the most photographed cottages in the area
with its sculptured hedges
Chipping Campden High Street is dominated by the old Covered Wool Market.
Built in 1627.
The adjacent Town Hall , has parts of the main building constructed in the 14th Century.
There is a splendid Church with an impressive tower. Opposite was a magnificent Jacobean
Manor House alas part destroyed in the Civil War skirmishes. Only the banqueting hall remains
The High Street now boasts arts and crafts studios along with antique and second hand book shops.
High class Hotels and Restaurants mingle with fine stone houses.
If you walk up to Dovers Hill, this is the edge of the escarpment of the Cotswolds affording you
fantastic views over Gloucestershire, Evesham and Tewkesbury.
This is also the start of The Cotswold Way Long Distance Trail . A ramble of over 100 miles to Bath
Dover Hill is also the site of the annual Cotswold Olympics held on the Spring Bank Holiday Friday.
Morris Dancing, Tug of War, Shin Kicking are just a few attractions.
Closing with a flaming torch procession back to the town later in the evening.

Now off to Broadway

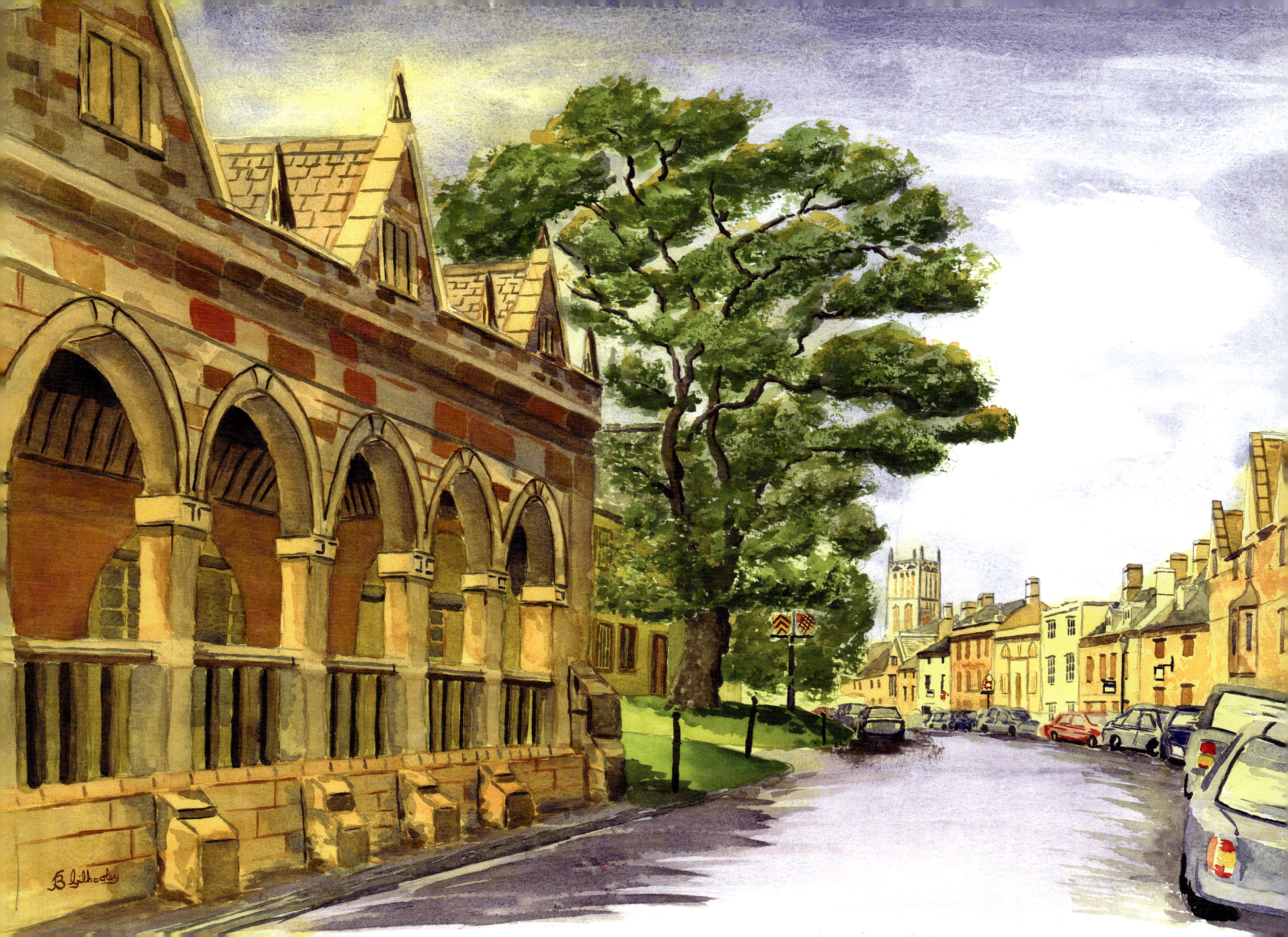

Broadway

Journeying further southwards there is Broadway another popular, now large village.
As the name suggests, the high street is wide with neat grass verges between the road and foot paths.
The famous Lygon Arms Hotel bearing the name of a General in the Battle of Waterloo
is to be found in the High Street
Visited by many of the rich and famous. 1885-86 John Singer Sargent Impressionist Artist
took up residence here. Some of his contemporaries lived locally.
The early 19th century was popular with landscape artists painting the surrounding area.
High Class Fine-Art Galleries grace the High street today, with Souvenir shops and Tea Rooms.
The Horse and Hound is one of the popular Inns for good food.

Following south on the route of the Cotswold Way you come to Snowshill.

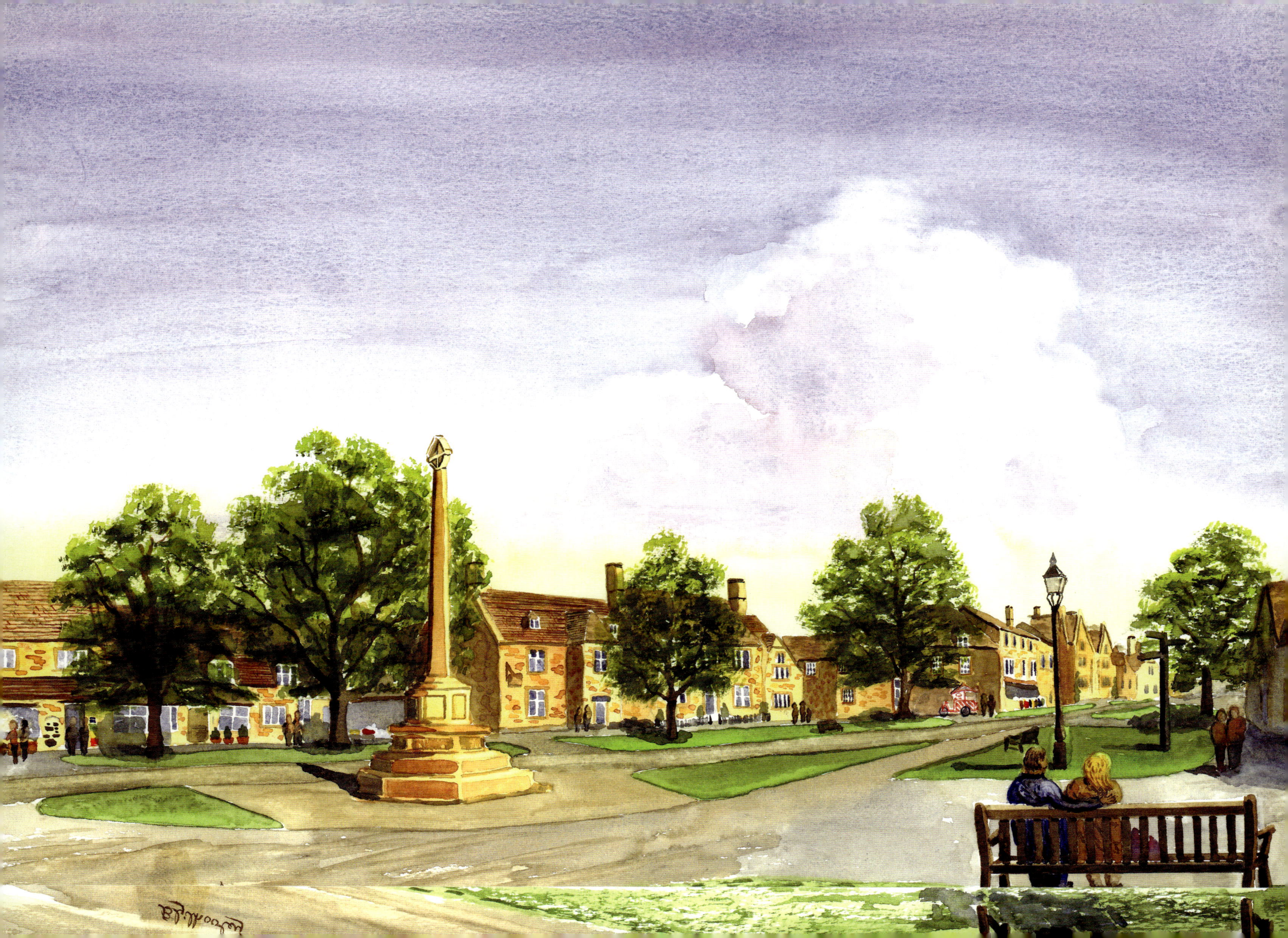

Snowshill

From the Campdens and Broadway we go south following the escarpment to the village of Snowshill.
Here you will find Snowshill Manor. Once owned by Charles Paget Wade an eccentric collector.
All things mechanical excited him. Musical instruments. Clocks ,Bicycles ,Toys and Japanese Armour
The house is now a National Trust property
The village is another collection of houses clinging to the hillside.
Higeldy pigeldy golden limestone cottages with the traditional split limestone tiled roofs
keeping the harsh prevailing Cotswold weather out.
But in the sunshine. How Picturesque!
As with many villages in the Cotswolds the prosperity of the labouring families fluctuated from a meagre subsistence to near starvation.
Most families lived off the land with hunger always knocking on the door and property in poor repair.
Unlike today where a lot of properties are second homes or holiday lets and are of a high quality restoration.
Here you can come off the Cotswold Way. visit the village take a meal in the Snowshill Arms pub.
then rejoin to ramble on.

Moving ever southwards are the villages of Stanton and Stanway

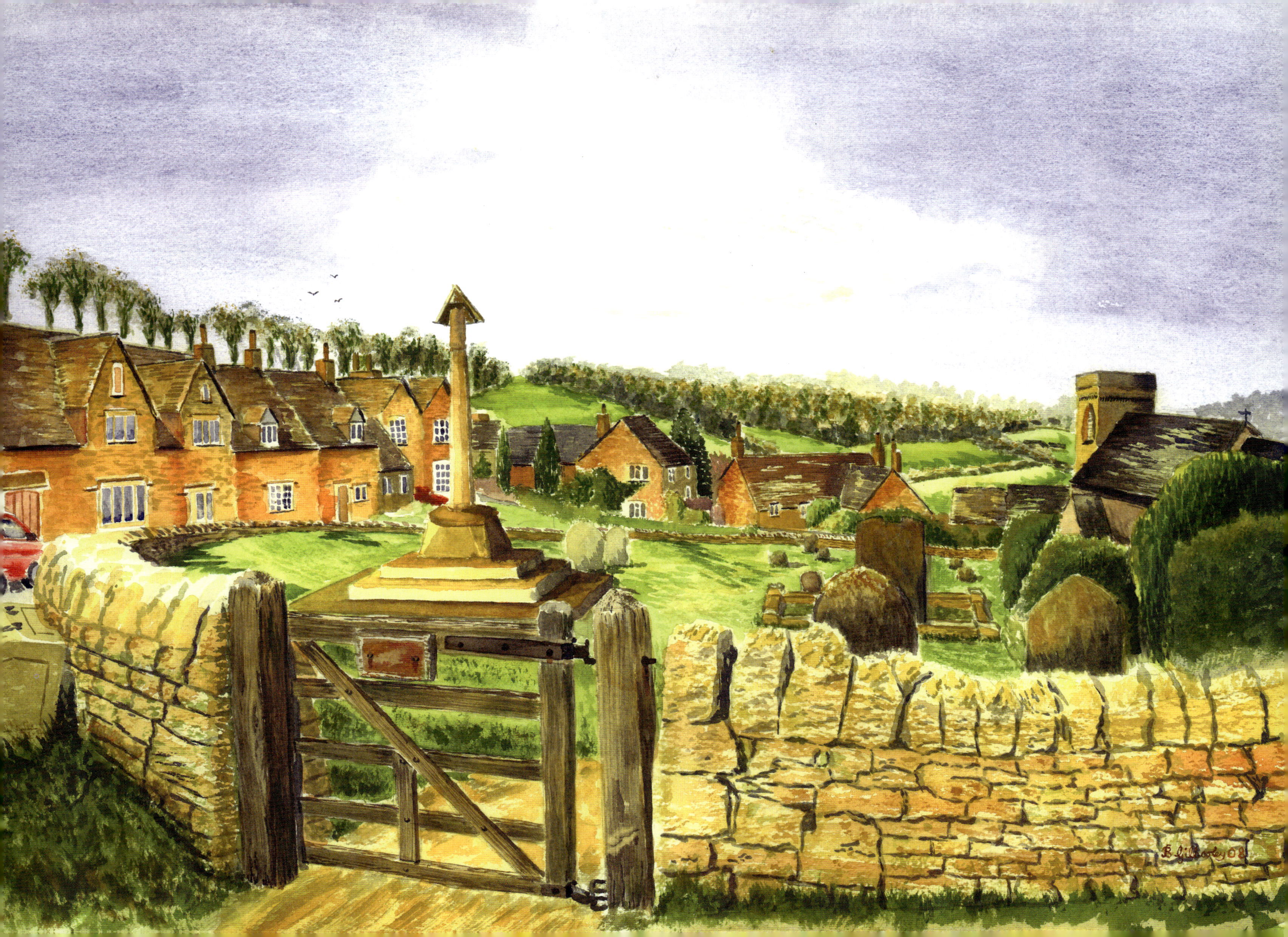

Stanton

Close to Snowshill is Stanton with it's stone cottages lining either side of the high street
and leading up hill to the Green with its Stott Lantern light.
The village has been used in films and TV sets.
Walking up higher to the top of the road is The Mount Inn surveying over its village.
And very popular it is too in the summer.
Part of the Cotswold way passes through the village.

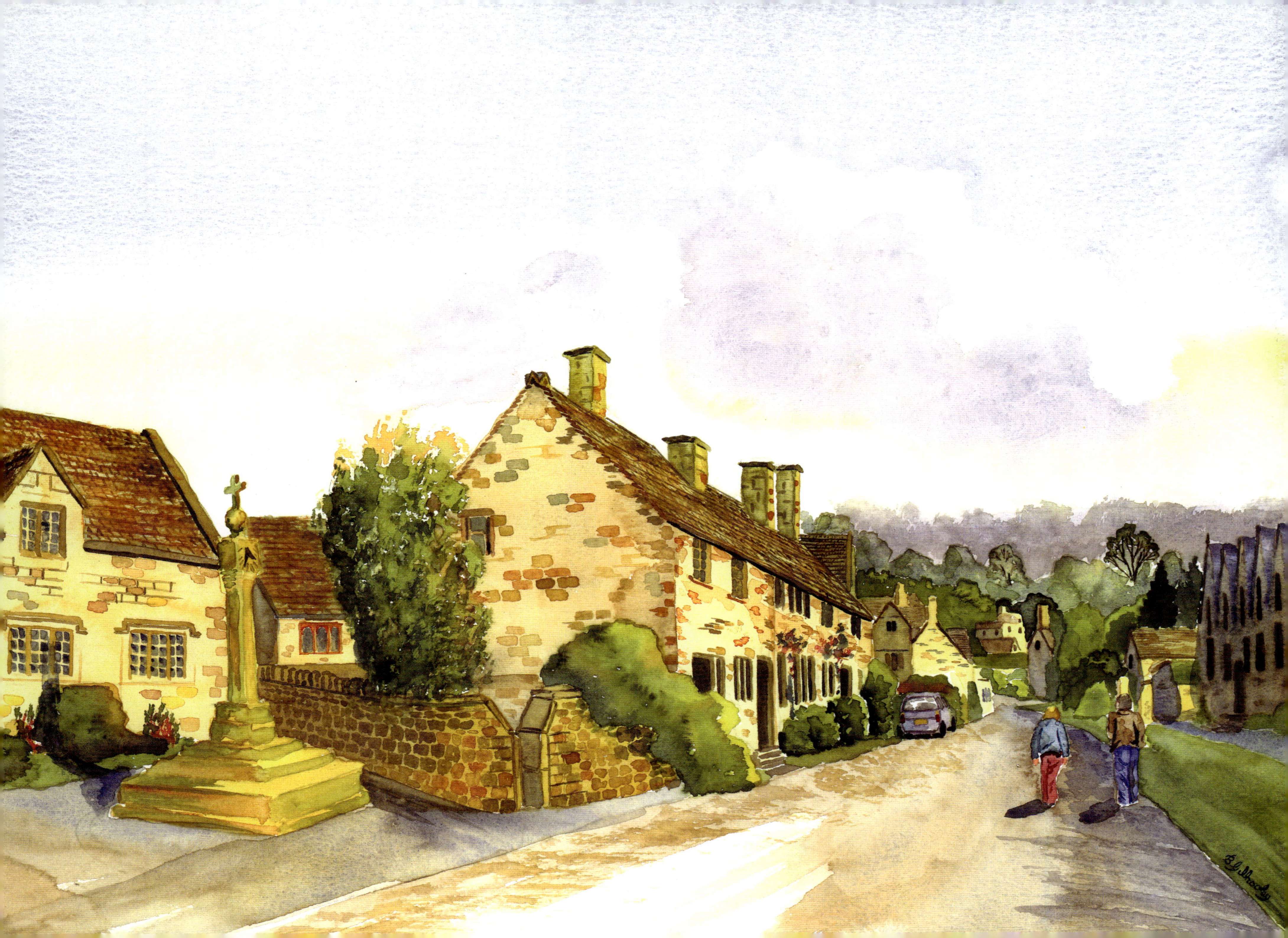

Stanway

Stanway is worth mentioning as it has a splendid Manor house and gate way.
Just beyond the gate way is a fullers mill, employed in wool processing.
Although partly derelict, it is now under renovation and it is hoped open to the public shortly
At the side of the Manor is a cricket pitch with an unusual and fine pavilion.
it's of timber construction on Stadle stone footings with a fine thatch roof.

On our journey south we next come to Hailes Abbey

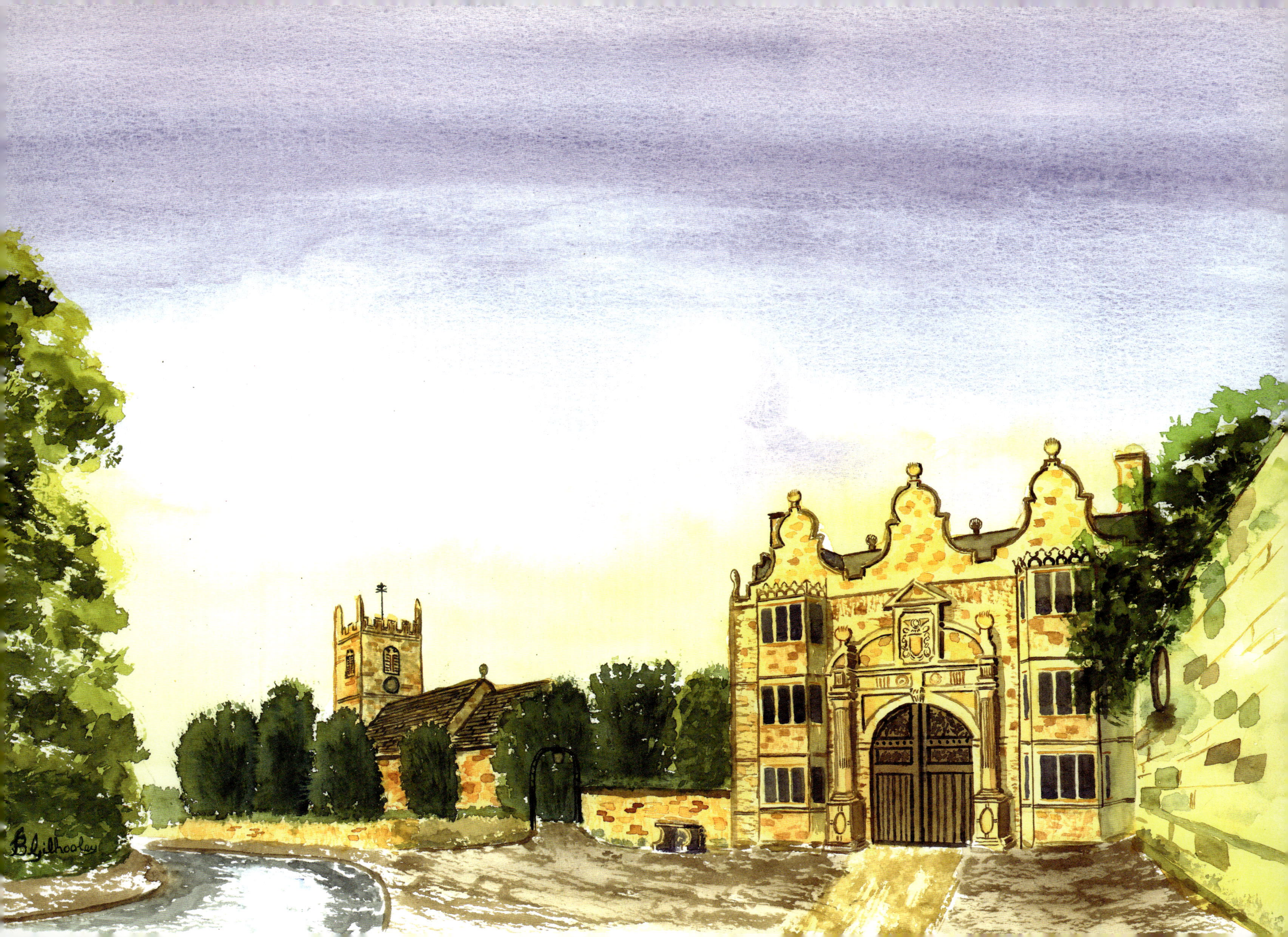
B.Gilhooley

Hailes Abbey

In its Hey-day It must have been one of the most ore inspiring and breath taking constructions in the area.
With a magnificent lofty Cathedral like Church. Built in the middle part of the 12 00s.
Completed around 1280.
The monies to build the Abbey came from Richard Earl of Cornwall and brother to King Henry III
In a tremendous storm off Lands End in the Atlantic. Richard Vowed in his prayers. If the Lord God Saved his life he would fund a church in thanksgiving. The Abbey was begun. In 1245 A Cistercian Abbot. 30 Monks and Lay Brothers set up the order. Fortunes were very meagre until 1270 when A son of Richard brought a phial of The Holy Blood of Christ. from Europe.
This began a nationwide pilgrimage to the Abbey.
Although the prosperity of the abbey fluctuated from time to time as did the nearby town of Winchcombe.
The abbey continued until the 1540s with the Dissolution of the Monasteries .
The land was then taken by the Crown. The Church and some of the buildings were destroyed.
Part of the remainder converted into a Manor house. until the 17th Century.
A rather plane village chapel opposite the site is still a plain of worship.
The Abbey ruins are now tended by English Heritage.

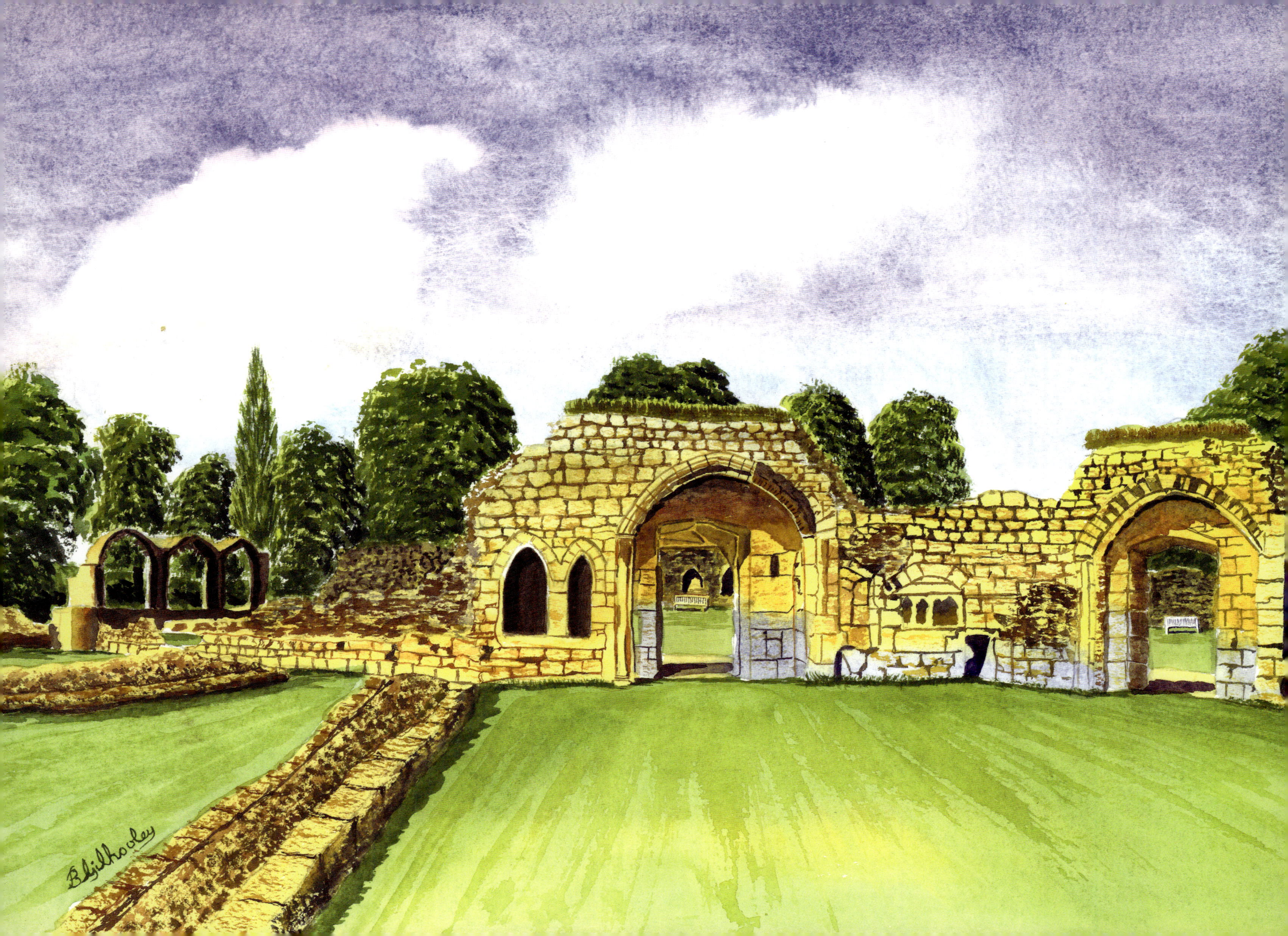

Winchcombe

Winchcombe of Winchcombeshire played many a part in history through out the ages.
Within close proximity of the town are two Roman Villas.
In the Anglo-Saxon times Winchcombe was once the capital of Mercia
With its own King. "King Kenulf."
The King played a part in setting up a Benedictine Abbey in the town in around 790.
A second abbey was established 3 miles outside the town.
A thriving Cistercian Abbey at Hailes, until its destruction in the
Dissolution of the Monasteries 1540. It is a tranquil spot today.
On the edge of the town is Sudeley Castle. Another must see.
Full of history! Some weekends having a special themed weekend
It is open to the public from April to November.
Henry the eighth's wife Catherine Parr lived in the area.
She is buried in the chapel adjacent to the castle.
The Castle is a fine example with the Ashcome Family still in residence.
Winchcombe itself is a bustling town of narrow streets, Antique Shops, Galleries
Tea Rooms and old Coaching inns.
The Old Corner Cupboard is an early coaching inn with an unusual name and history.

We leave Winchcombe and go across country to Ford.

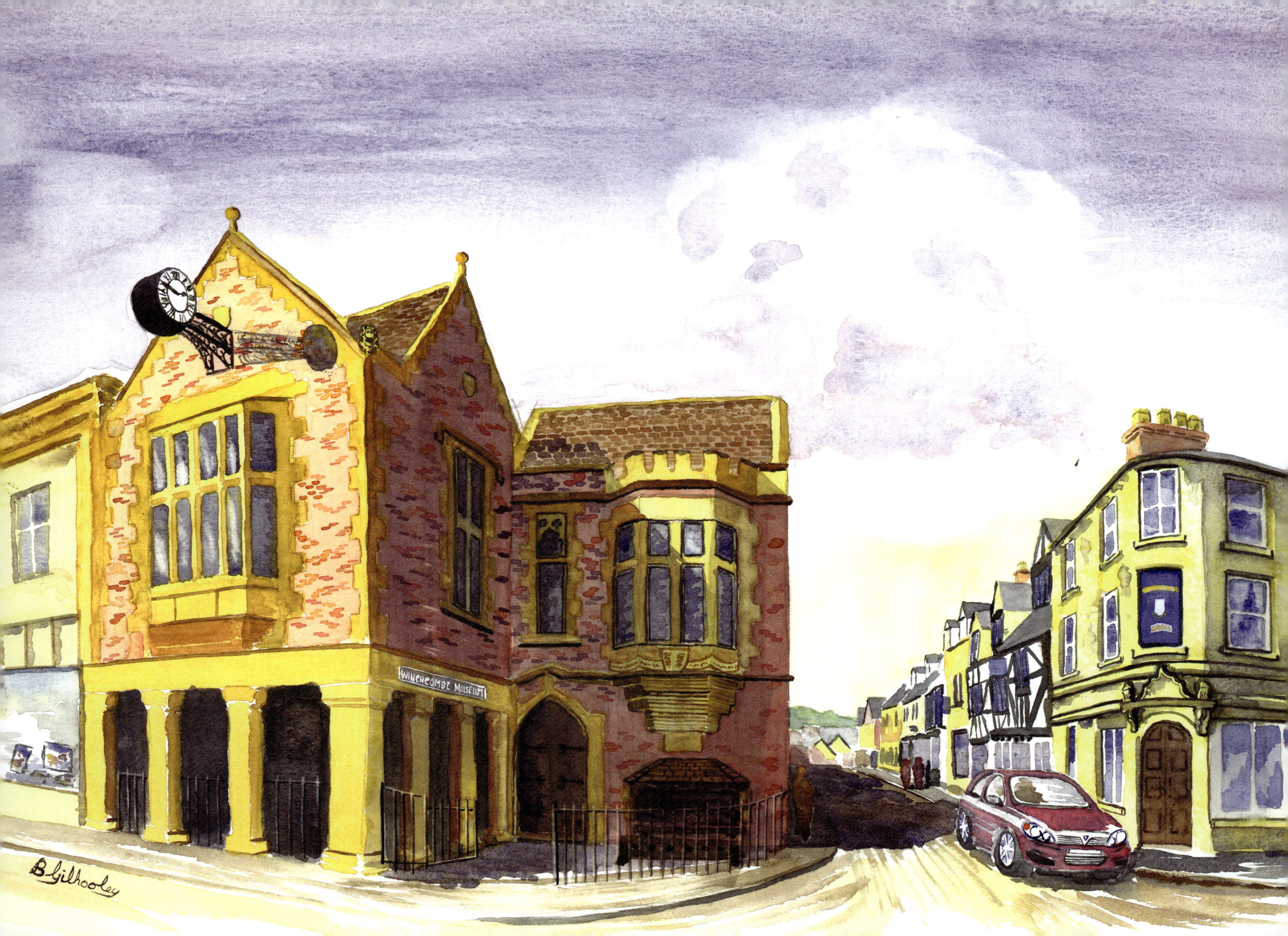
WINCHCOMBE MUSEUM
B.Gilhooley

Ford

A small village on the busy B4077 between Stow and Tewkesbury.
It is the heart of the horse racing area in the North Cotswolds
With a leading national horse training stables in the village.
The Local pub as you can imagine is a buzz of every thing horsey.
Looking out of the windows of the pub straight onto the gallops.
The food is of a high standard and an absolute winner too!
This painting overlooks the village to the Gallops.

A little way off to the south are the Guitings.

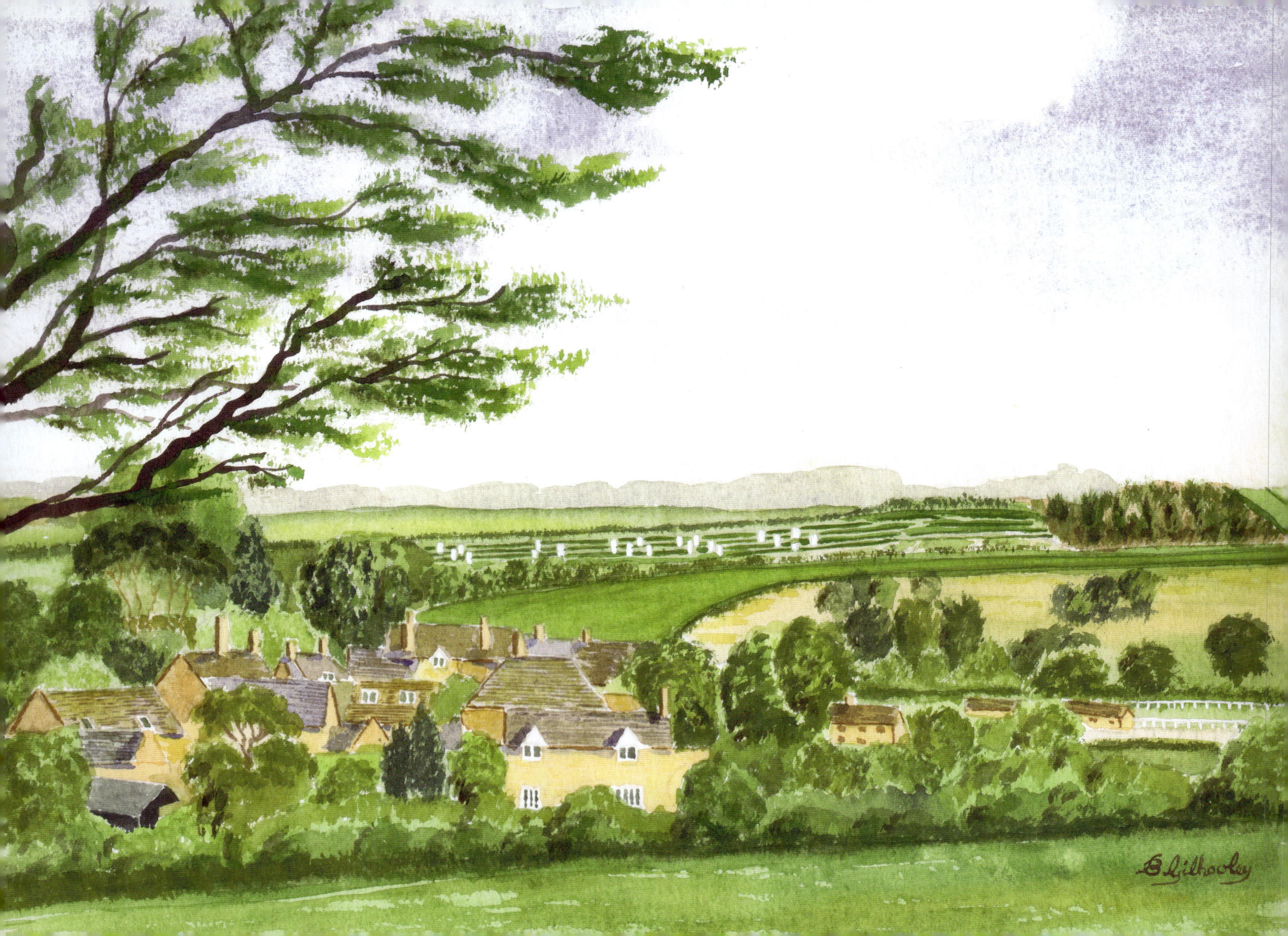

Temple Guiting

Just south of Ford in a wooded valley is Temple Guiting, a quiet village.
Although small it still has a shop and a village School
The impressive Church and Manor House have connections with the
Knight Templars of the 12 century, Holy - Land Crusades.
King Richard the Lion Hart and all that.
The land around was owned by the Templer's at that time.
The Manor is a fine example of Tudor Architecture.
It has limited opening to the public.
The name Guiting is old English relating to water, possibly a spring or river.

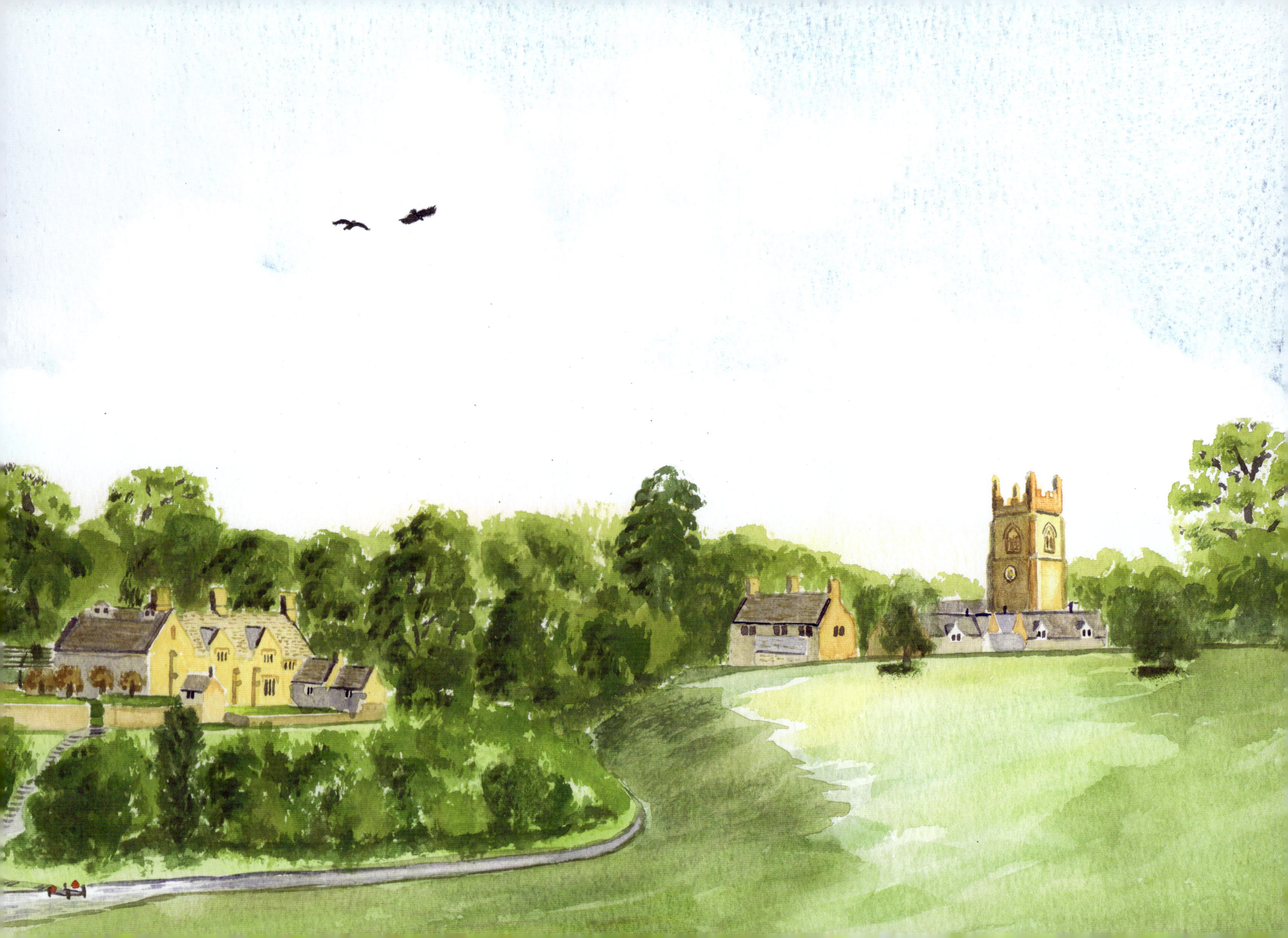

Guiting Power

The big sister to the other Guiting village is a quintessential Cotswold village
Pretty unspoilt cottages, village green. Shop and two pubs.
The church is a short walk to the south end of the village.
It has a splendid Norman doorway.
Near half of the village and the church was lost to dereliction in the late
1890s –1900s due to poverty once the sheep trade fell into decline.
Now like many villages resurrected and pristine
Of the two pubs the Hollow Bottom Inn to the north end of the village
was until recently owned by a leading jockey Peter Scudamore in
partnership with a well known trainer. The pub is full of racing memorabilia
And is regularly frequented by people in the Game!
Painting the Green was a lovely sunny afternoon.
A Local dog appeared part way through and trotted over tail wagging to see what I was doing.

We now go ever eastwards to the Slaughters

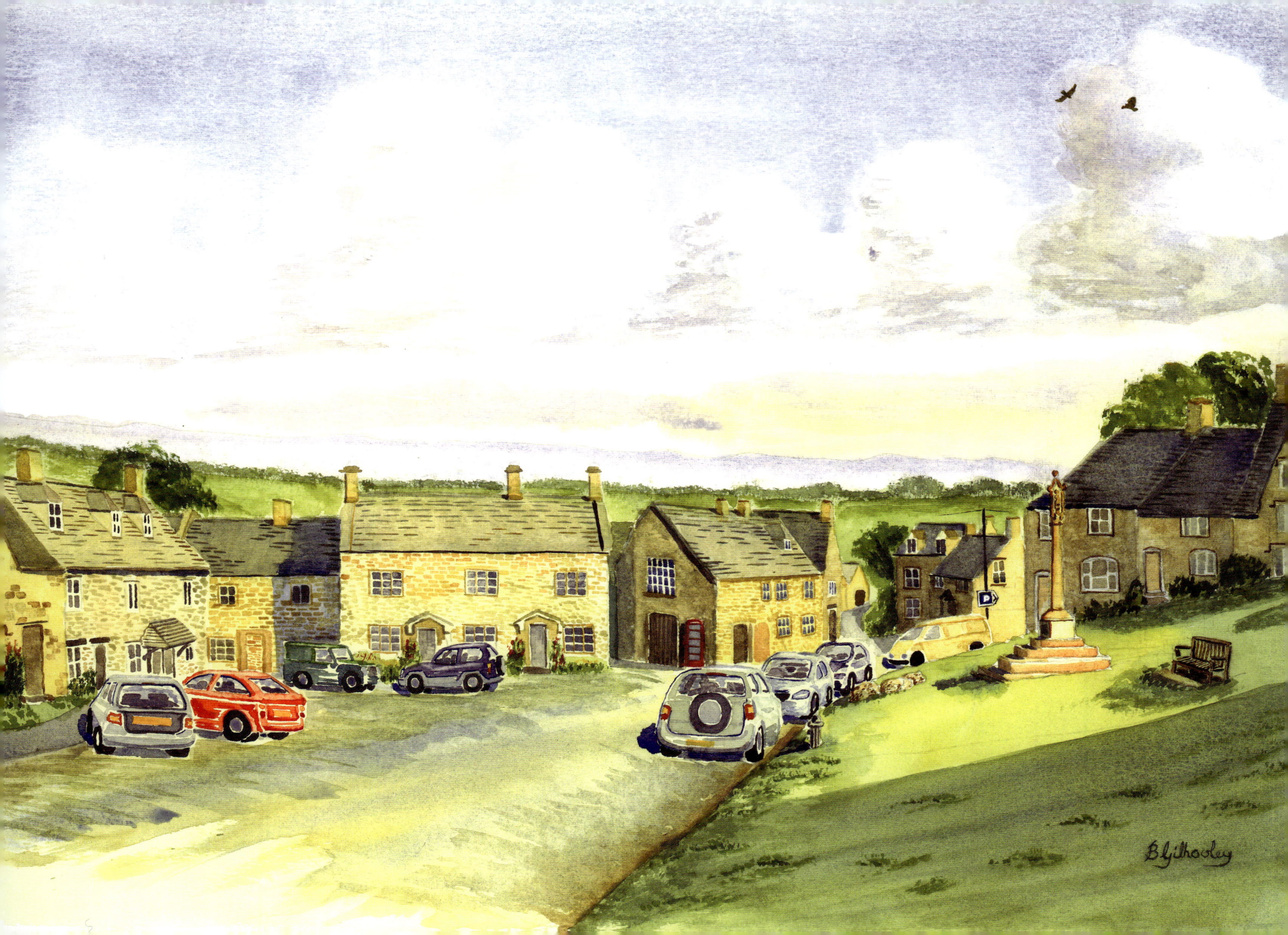

P
B Gilhooley

Upper Slaughter

These are two pretty little villages The upper and lower Slaughter linked by the small river Eye meandering through the valley.
The word slaughter again Saxon and does not have sinister meanings.
Translating as muddy and probably relates to the ford.
There is a shallow ford across the river in Upper Slaughter and well worth a stroll.
Many visitors park up and enjoy the gentle stroll from one village to the other.
The more adventurous can walk the Heart of England Way through to Bourton.
In Upper Slaughter there is the remains of a Norman fort with a Motte and Bailey.
With the battle of Donnington in the Civil War close by.
a further skirmish took place in Upper Slaughter.

We leave this now peaceful village and go down stream to Lower Slaughter.

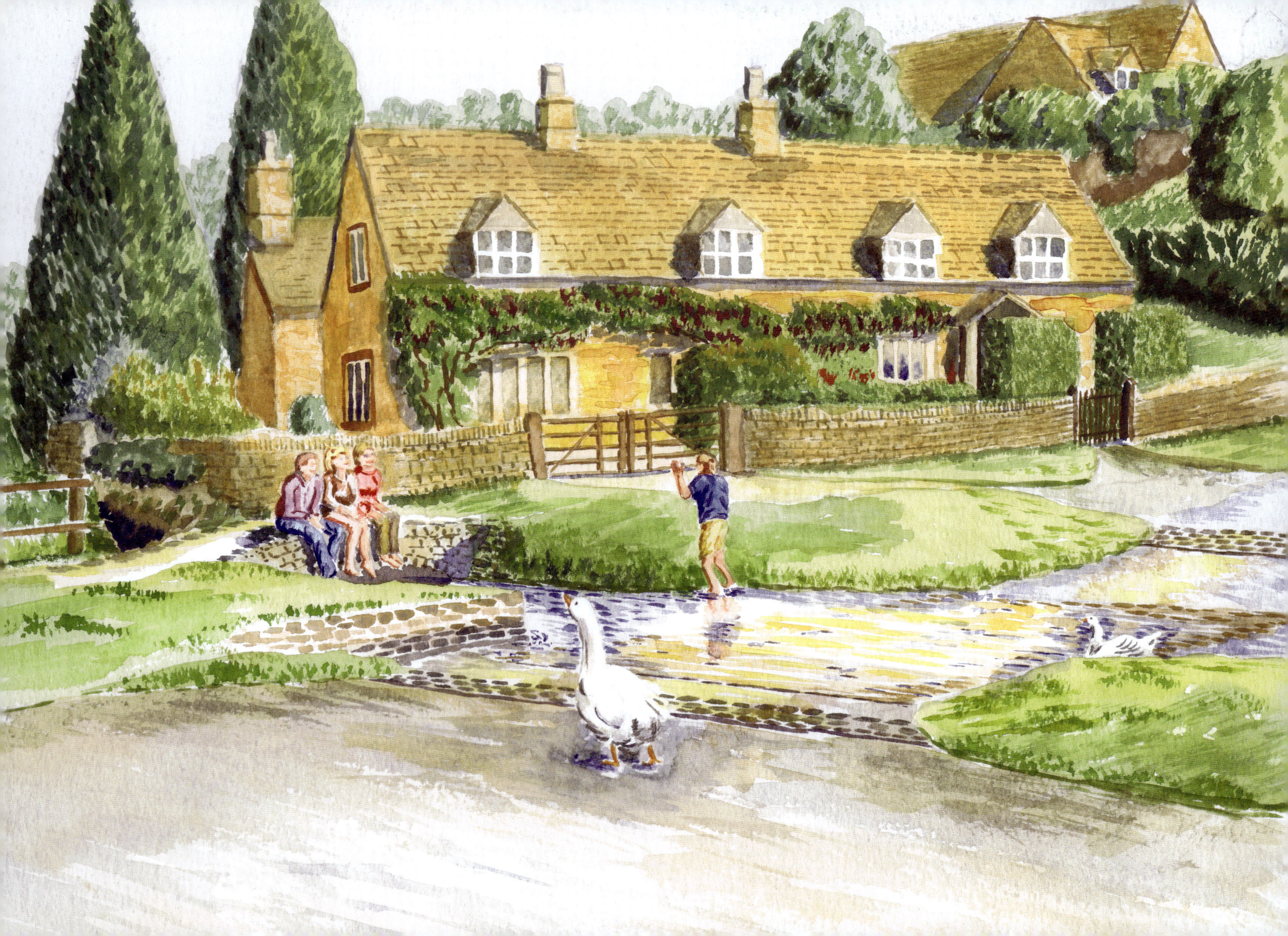

Lower Slaughter

This is almost a too manicured and perfectly picturesque village.
Its twee cottages either side of the stream and roadway sit perfectly proportioned, connected either side by low stone foot bridges. Fish dart up and down the crystal clear stream with Mallard ducks, some paddling others sleeping on the grassy river banks enjoying the summer sun.
At the head of this village is the Old Mill. Now part museum part Tea Room, part Shop & part Tourist Office.
The local lime stone in this area is of high quality and was used on the colleges in Oxford, some taken by cart, then sent down the Thames was used in prominent buildings in London.
Both Villages are built of local quarried stone, but unusual for this area the end wall and tall chimney of the mill is constructed in red brick.
The village hall in Lower Slaughter plays host to many Art and Craft Exhibitions through out the summer.

Moving further south we cross the busy Fosse Way to Bourton on the Water.

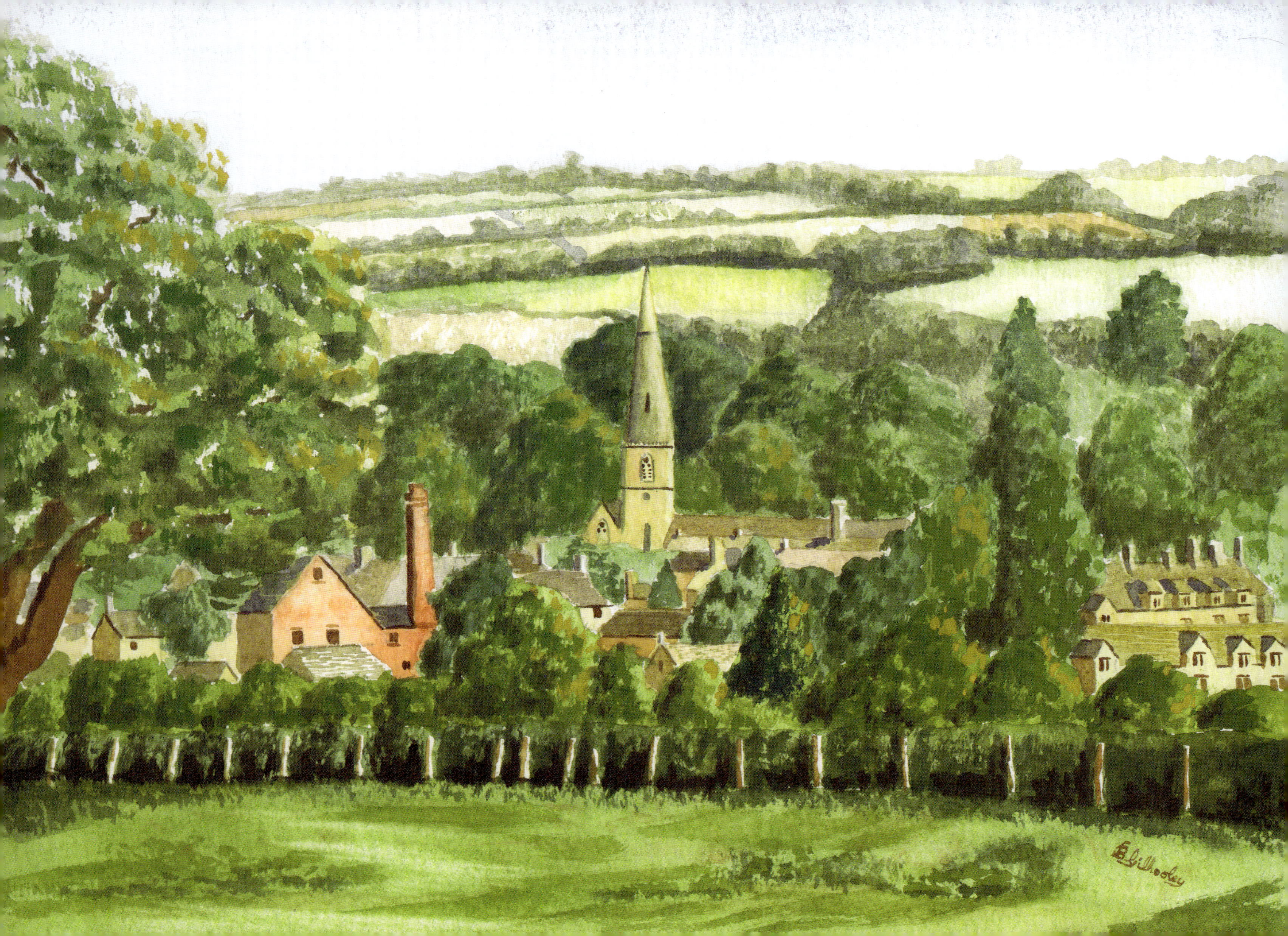

Bourton on the water

Little Venice of the Cotswolds this is a Very popular picturesque Village in the North Cotswolds.
There was a Roman settlement here by the river. Iron Age, to the Anglo Saxons have all favoured this area.
Renowned for the clear shallow Windrush River with it's series of foot bridges and ford.
In the summer it is a mecca for day trippers.
Unfortunately I find Bank Holidays are unbearable here.
The whole village is geared up for the tourist with Bird Land, Model Village and Car museum,
Perfumery, Nick-knack shops & Tea rooms etc.
However mid-week it is still worth visiting.

A Little west of Bourton just off the A436 is Salperton

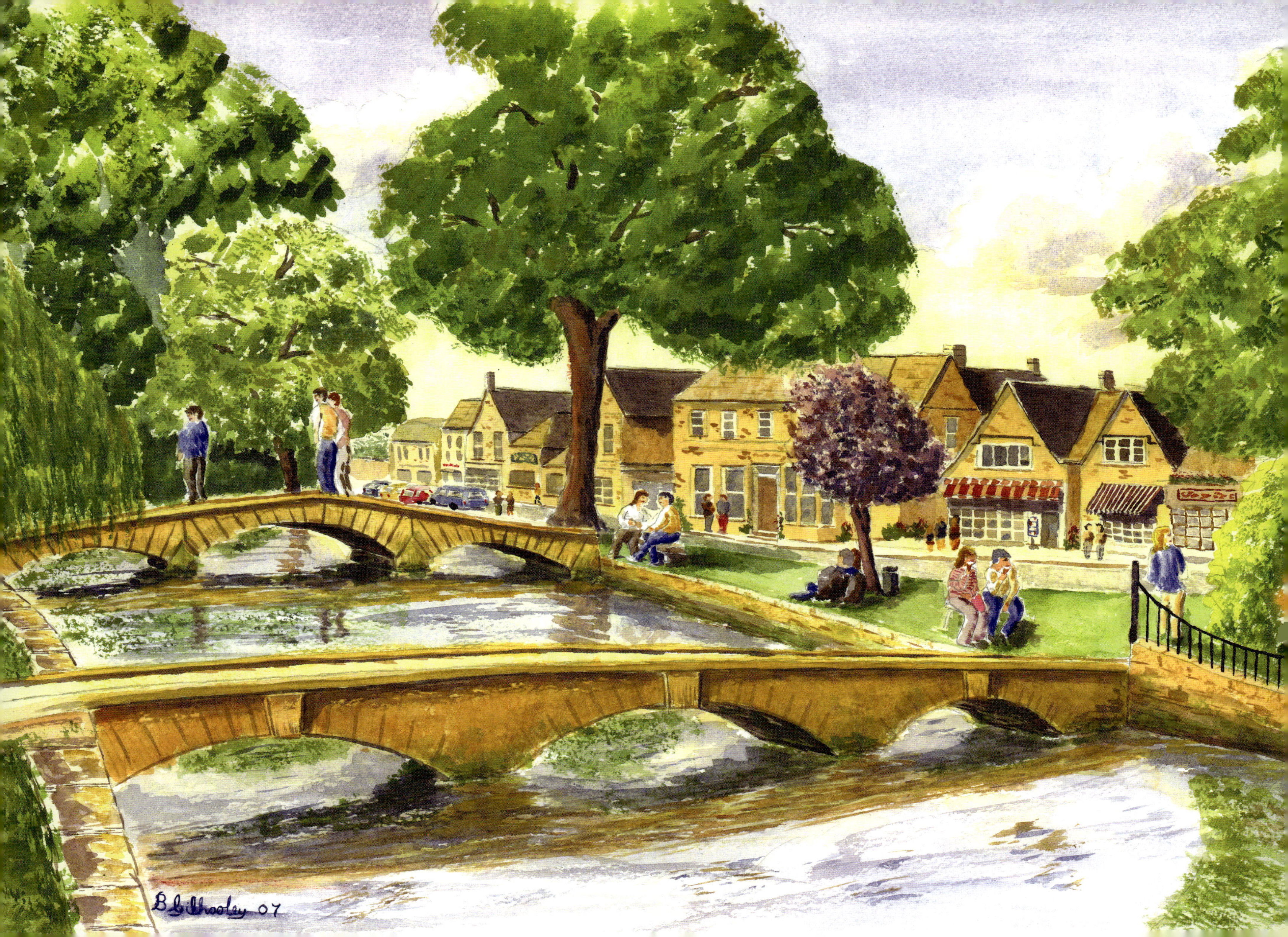
B Gilhooley 07

Salperton

Another sleepy little village. A row of neat and pretty cottages overlook a babbling brook and water meadow, with hills in the background just made a perfect view for me to put onto paper. Around the corner is another collection of cottages and long stone barn nestling together.
The village was mentioned in the Domesday Book, at that time it had a Knight . Sir Thomas Comyn overseeing its well being.
With its proximity to the old salt ways, it is believed the village name may be a corruption relating to salt.
Much later with the coming of the Railway. The line from Cheltenham and Gloucester. it is surprising the village did not grow.
The quietness now is what makes this village so charming.
Criss crossing this area are the Gloucester way and the Diamond way Long distance foot paths. Ideal for the ramblers among you.
Now we make our way south to visit the Roman villa at Chedworth. If you go by way of Compton Abdale Look out for the Crocodile by the cross roads? .

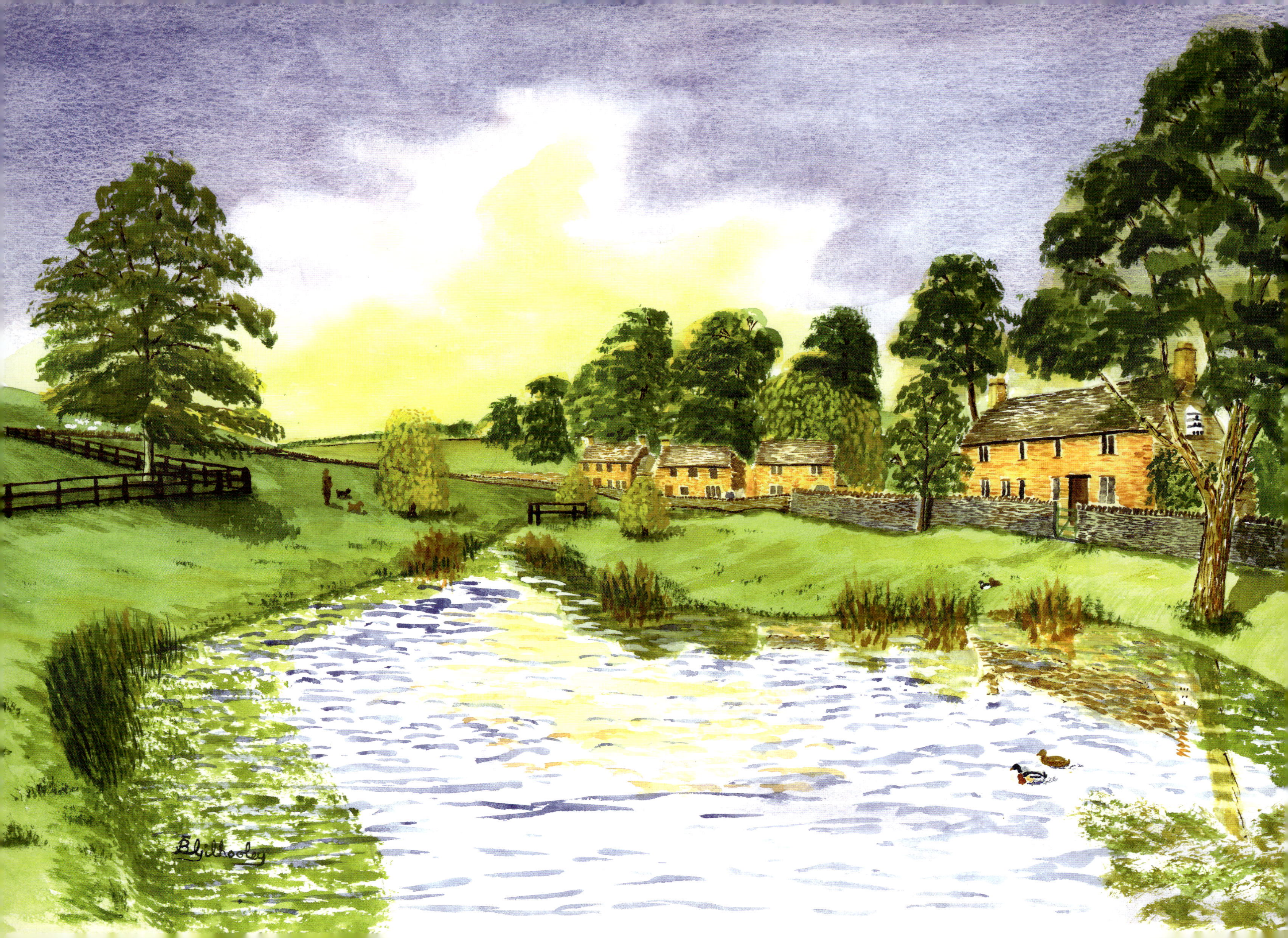

Chedworth Roman Villa

This whole area has many Roman connections. This villa is one of the best preserved and most accessible.
Set in a most beautiful wooded valley, the villa was investigated in the Victorian times.
Then having a Hunting Lodge built on the site.
Since then there have been many archaeological digs setup here.
Some buildings dating from 150 A.D. A water shrine, heated bath houses. Living rooms and kitchen etc
are all laid out for you to see, together with floor mosaics and paved walkways.
The whole site beautifully preserved with a very informative museum, gift shop and café.
The National Trust supervises the upkeep of this prime settlement..
There is a foot path, part of The Macmillan Way. Taking you through the woods to the present village of
Chedworth.

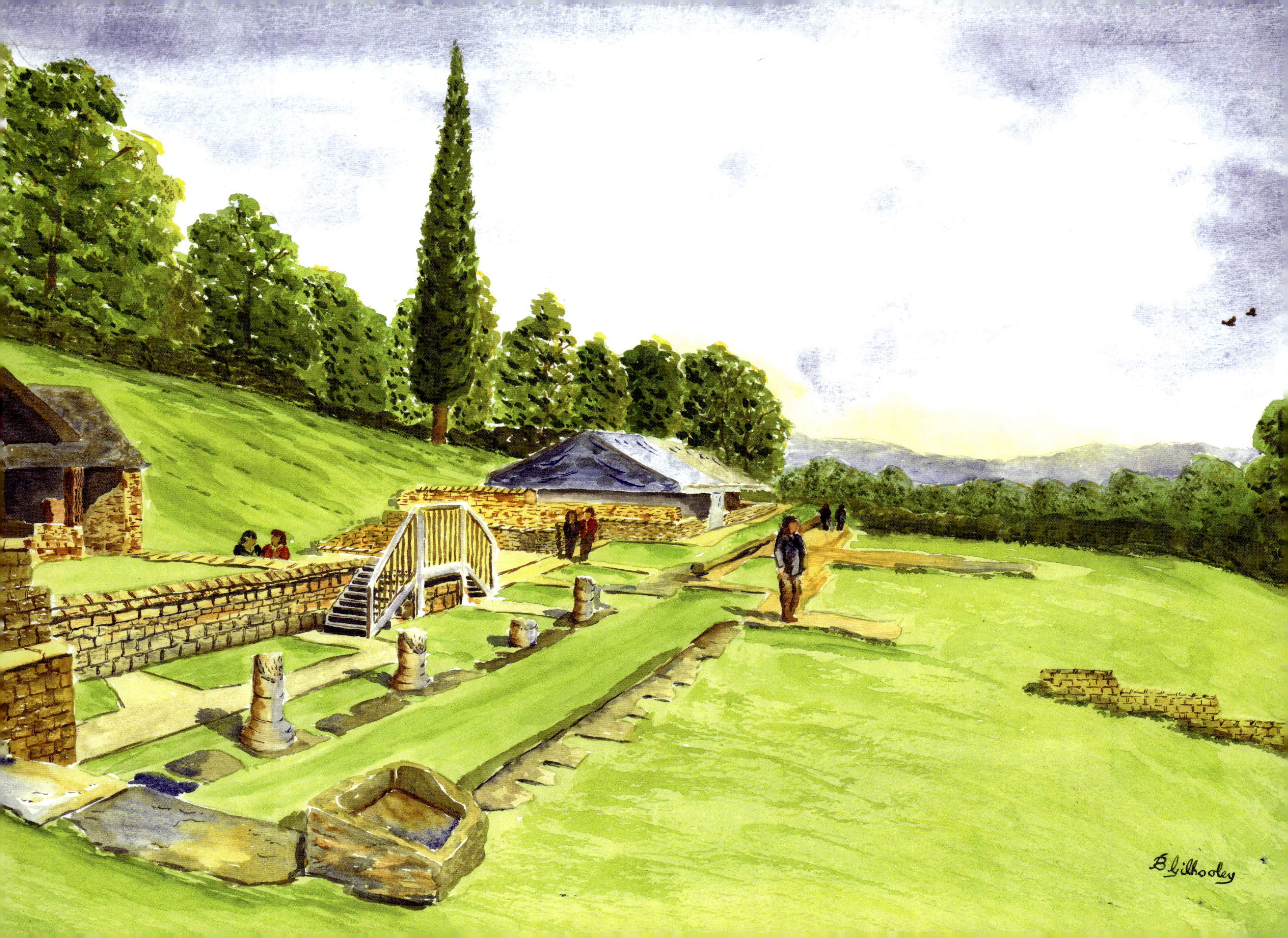
B Gilhooley

Chedworth Village

Set on the side of a valley.
This is a sprawling village along the hillside, with the centre at the northerly end the most picturesque.
Having the Church overlooking quaint stone cottages, higgledy pigaldy leading down to the village pub.
Another hidden gem.
The Seven Tuns Inn offers real Ales and recommended appetising cooking in a rustic atmosphere.
Across from the pub a babbling spring spurting out of the hill side adds to the quaintness of the village.
The Macmillan Way from Lincolnshire down to the Dorset coast, passes through the village together with the Monarch's Way.
The Macmillan Way is walked by many fund raisers for this fine cause.
Other foot paths take you along Hedgley Bottom to Fosse Bridge on the Fosse Way..

Head to the Fosse Way and to Northleach

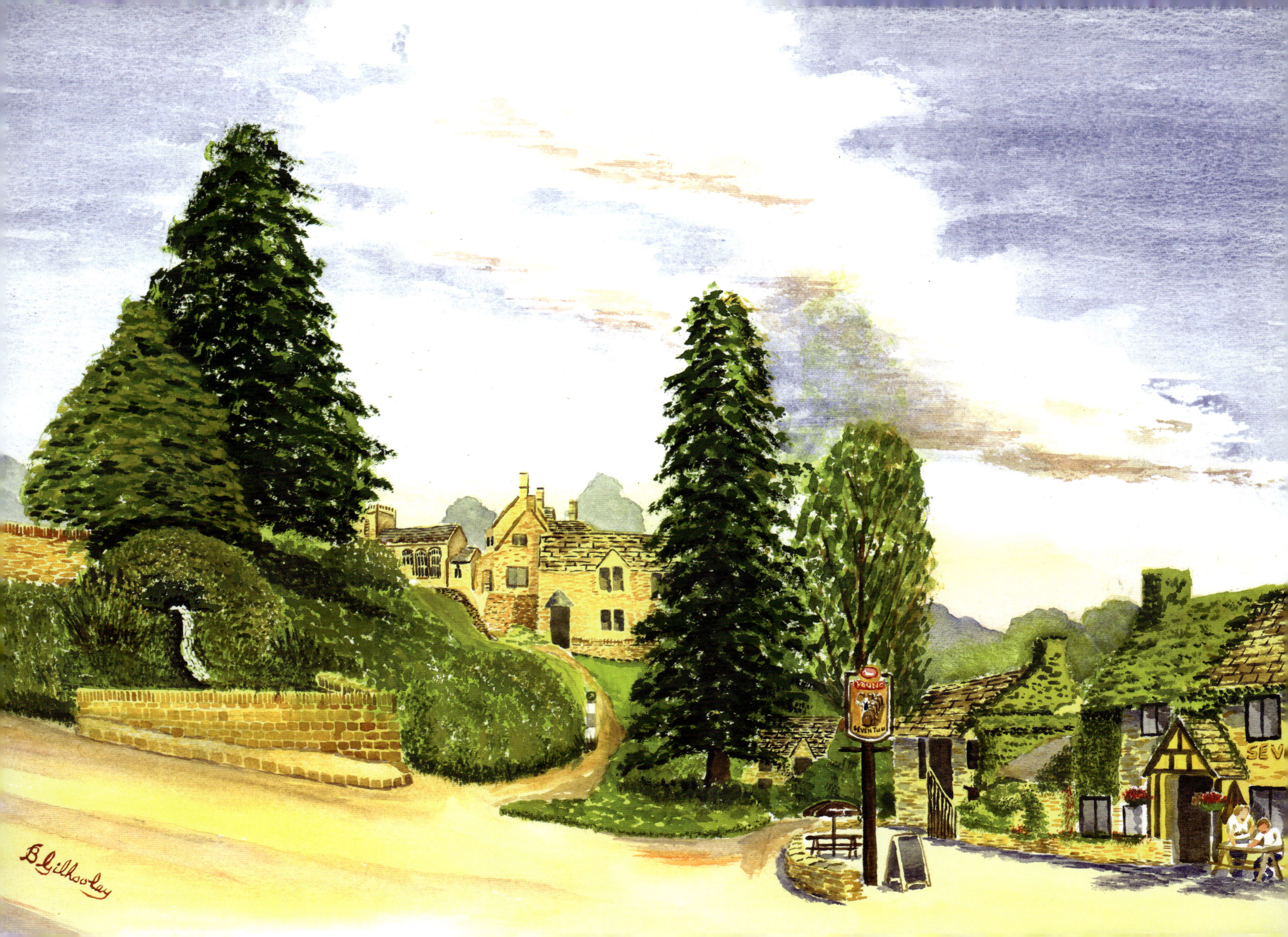
YOUNG
SEV
B Gilhooley

Northleach

On the Fosse Way the Romans of course marched past the town.
In the Middle Ages the salt way pack horses and wagoners came through .
Bringing Salt, mined in Droitwich through the town on their way to Lechlade.
Then journeying down by the river Thames to London.
The sheep markets of course, and in the 1800 and 1900s horse drawn coaches from London to Cheltenham and Gloucester brought prosperity to the town.
Unusual! on the Fosse is The Old Prison.
In the 18ct , when the prison was operating, Prisoners were held in small cells and employed turning a tread mill.
The layout of the prison was a model for a new range of Houses of Correction in the 1900 s such as Pentonville
In London The building has a more pleasant outlook today.
Now it is a delightful Blades Café offering locally sourced fresh cooked food.
The exercise yard has a collection of old farm machinery and some 40 farm carts. A unique country museum.
Another attraction in the town is an interesting museum of mechanical musical instruments.

We go across country now to Bibury.

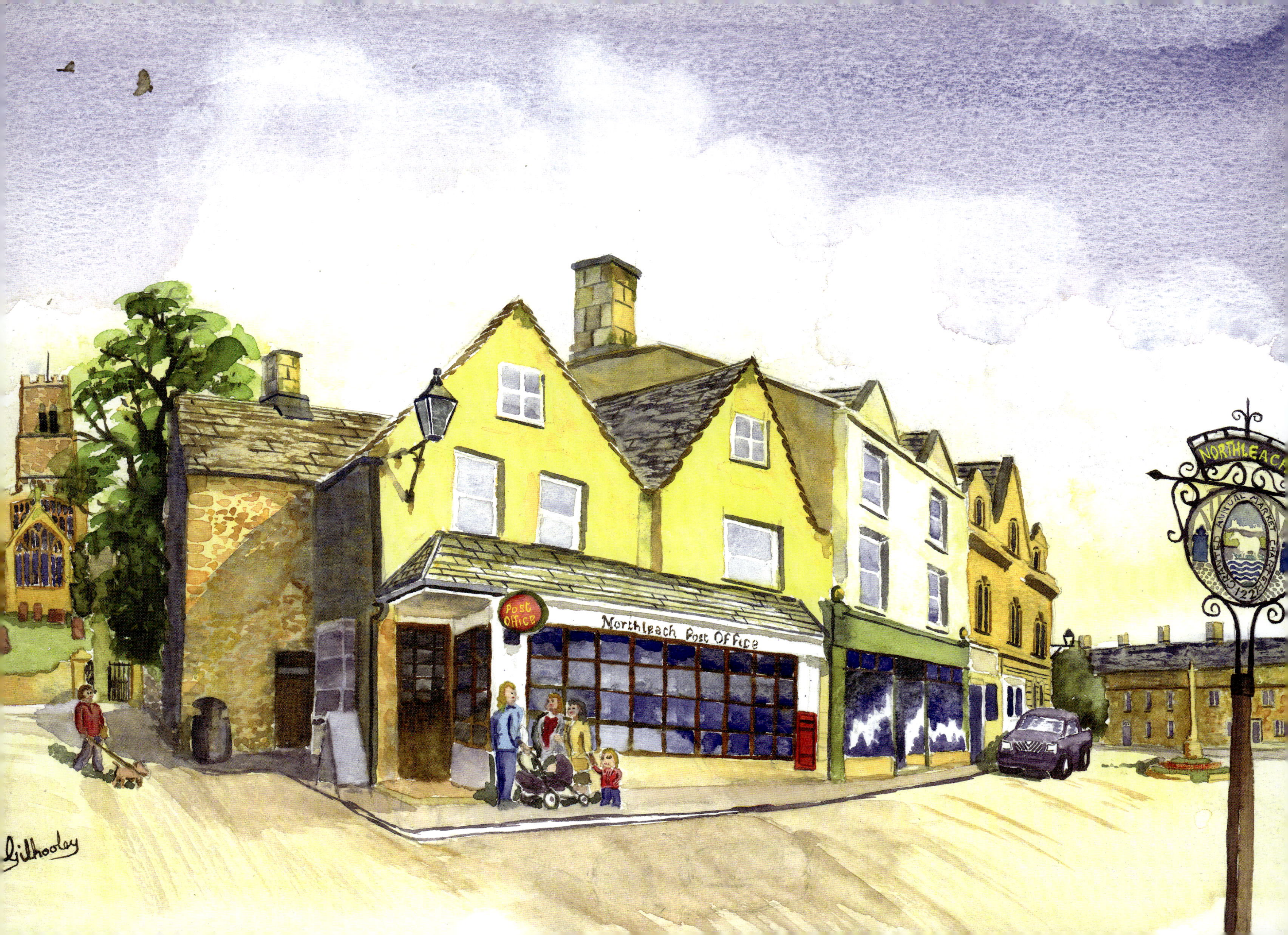
Post Office
Northleach Post Office

Bibury & Arlington Row

Situated on the river Coln. A clean and fast moving river.
This made an Ideal location in the Middle Ages for the treatment of wool.
Arlington Row by the river was a terrace of one up one down weavers cottages
No doubt in the 17th century a very hard life for the workers.
The husband working on the land or in the mill.
The wife spinning or weaving wool from daylight till dusk in the upstairs room.
Both having to raise a family in the ground floor one room accommodation.
The mill was also used for the treatment of wool.
Today the river still plays an important role in the village
There is a fish hatchery here. There is a thriving wet fish shop "Delicious !"
Or you can go and catch your own trout for tea.

Travelling on we go to Eastleach

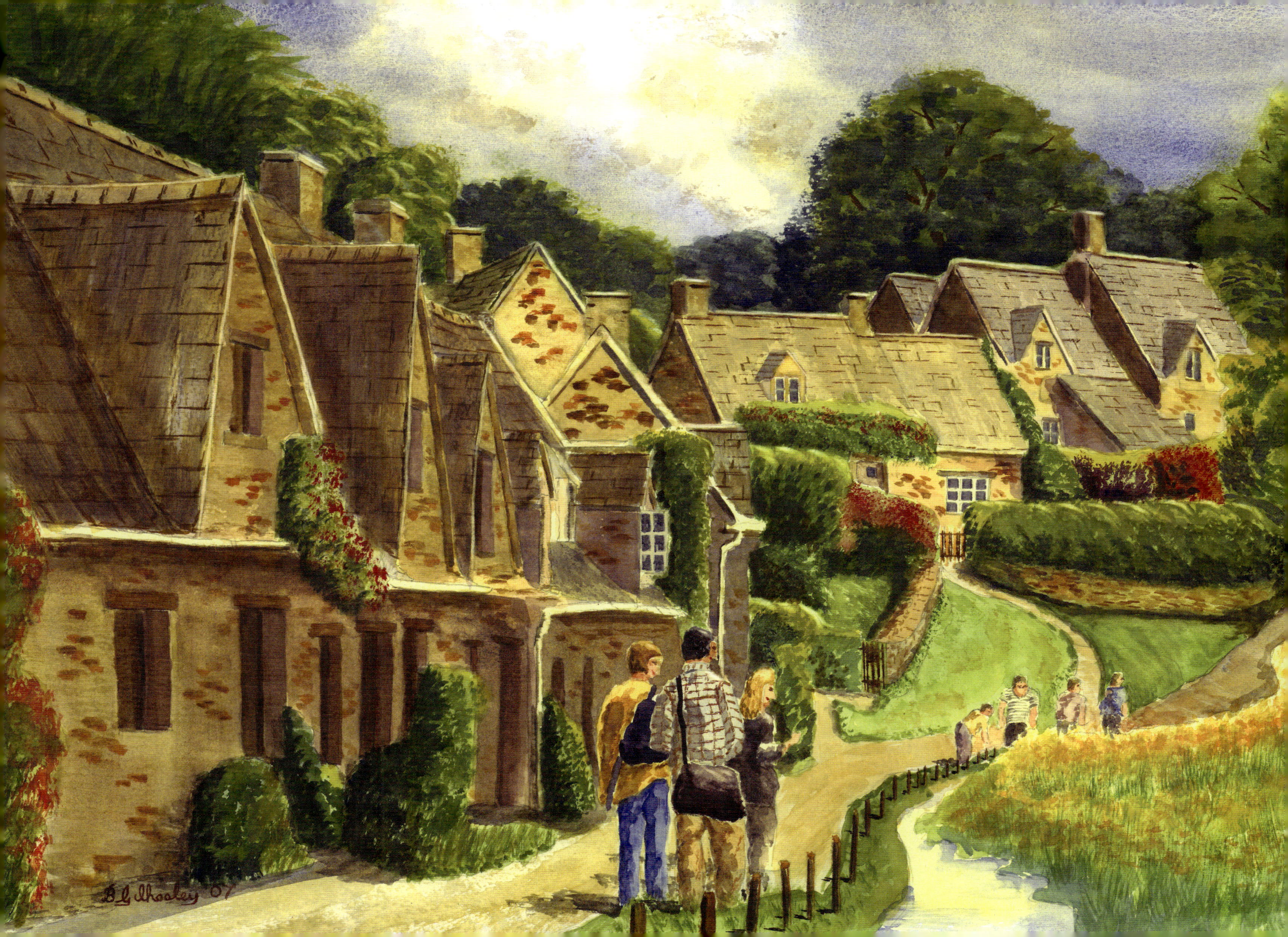

Eastleach Martin & Eastleach Turville

Two enchanting villages sit side by side with the river Leach separating them.
The villages are noted for the "Keble Flagstone Foot bridge " separating the two churches
Some 500 yards from one another
The Keble family were lords of the manor.
John Keble was an author and had connections with Keble College Oxford.
You can stop and refresh yourselves, whiling away an hour or two at the Victoria Inn
to the north of Eastleach Turville

Now we swing north to Burford.

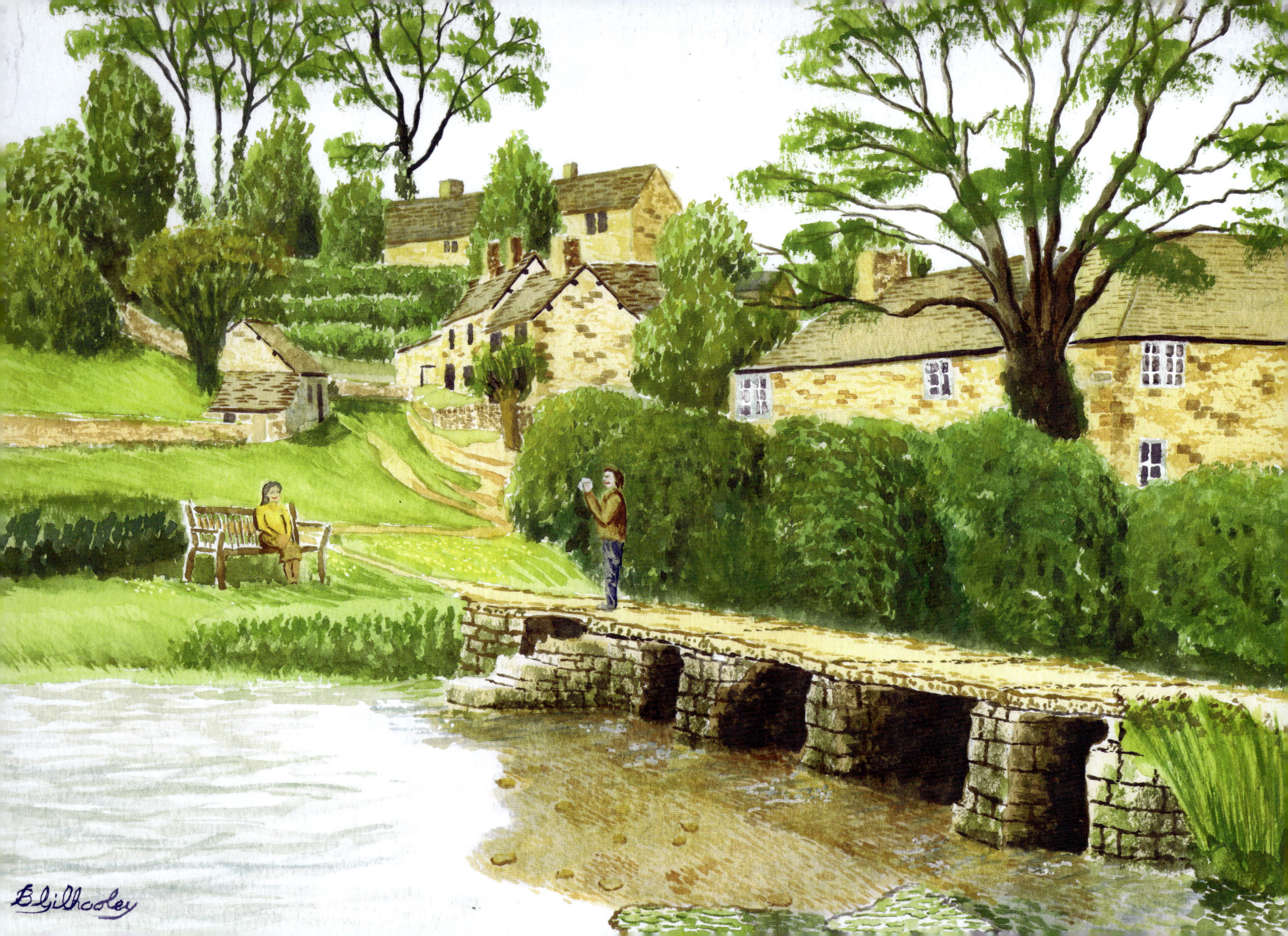
B.Gilhooley

Burford

A bustling town Burford has a very wide High Street coming down the side of a steep hill.
With the Church, Priory & School at it's foot beside the river Windrush.
A number of independent shops line either side of the High street
An important crossing point in the early days the ford and later bridge connected Stow
and the north to Lechlade and the south with the road from Oxford to Cirencester east to west.
It has one of the earliest markets granted in the 1100s.
Sheep Street and the Lamb Inn remind us of the importance to the prosperity of the town.
Burford remains a prosperous town today with a wealth of interesting
and unusual shops down the high street and well worth a stroll.

To the east of Burford we drive through Swinbrook to Minster Lovell

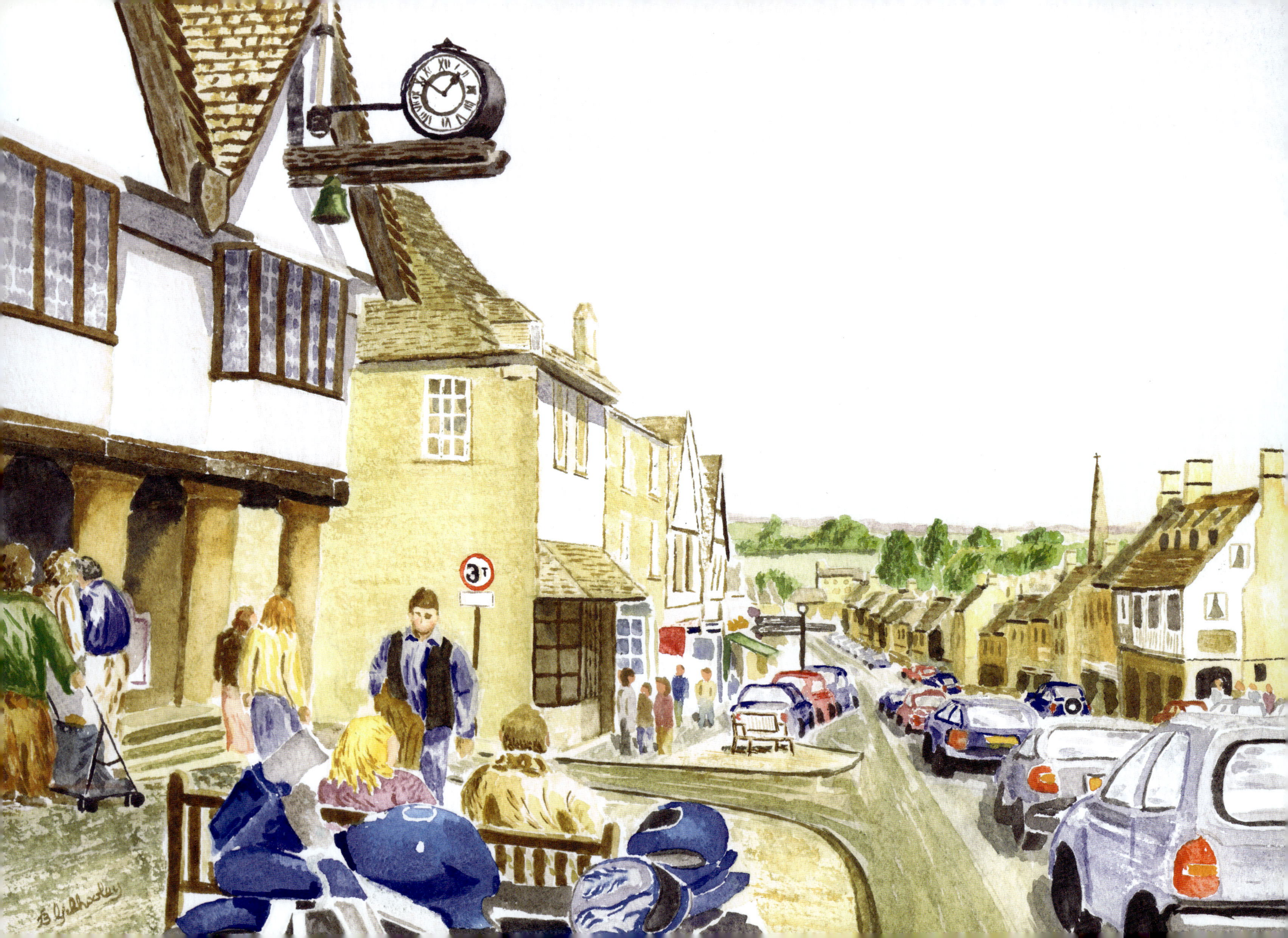
3T

Swinbrook

As I came into Swinbrook it was one of those artist moments.
I drove around the corner, and "There was a blaze of Golden Daffodils." A splash of colour I had to capture.
The small village has a brook running down from Seven Spring further north, through a small green,
under the road and joining the river Windrush a little to the south.
It was this Green in late March that stopped me.
Making use of a strategic park bench, I got out my paint tin and easel.
Sitting there taking it all in, the chill spring breeze brought me back to the job in question.
Here it is.
If you want to stretch your legs, a walk up to the church and beyond will take you across a field
to earth works. The site of the Medieval village of Widford.
A Little south of Swinbrook by the river Windrush is the Swan Inn. A pleasant place for refreshments.
I lately have learned of a legend about three brothers born here abouts.
In the mid 1700s they were notorious highwaymen. Their names, Tom, Dick and Harry. Are believed to be
the origins of the often used saying. They were caught and hung at nearby Shipton under Wychwood

Now off to Minster Lovell and its secret.

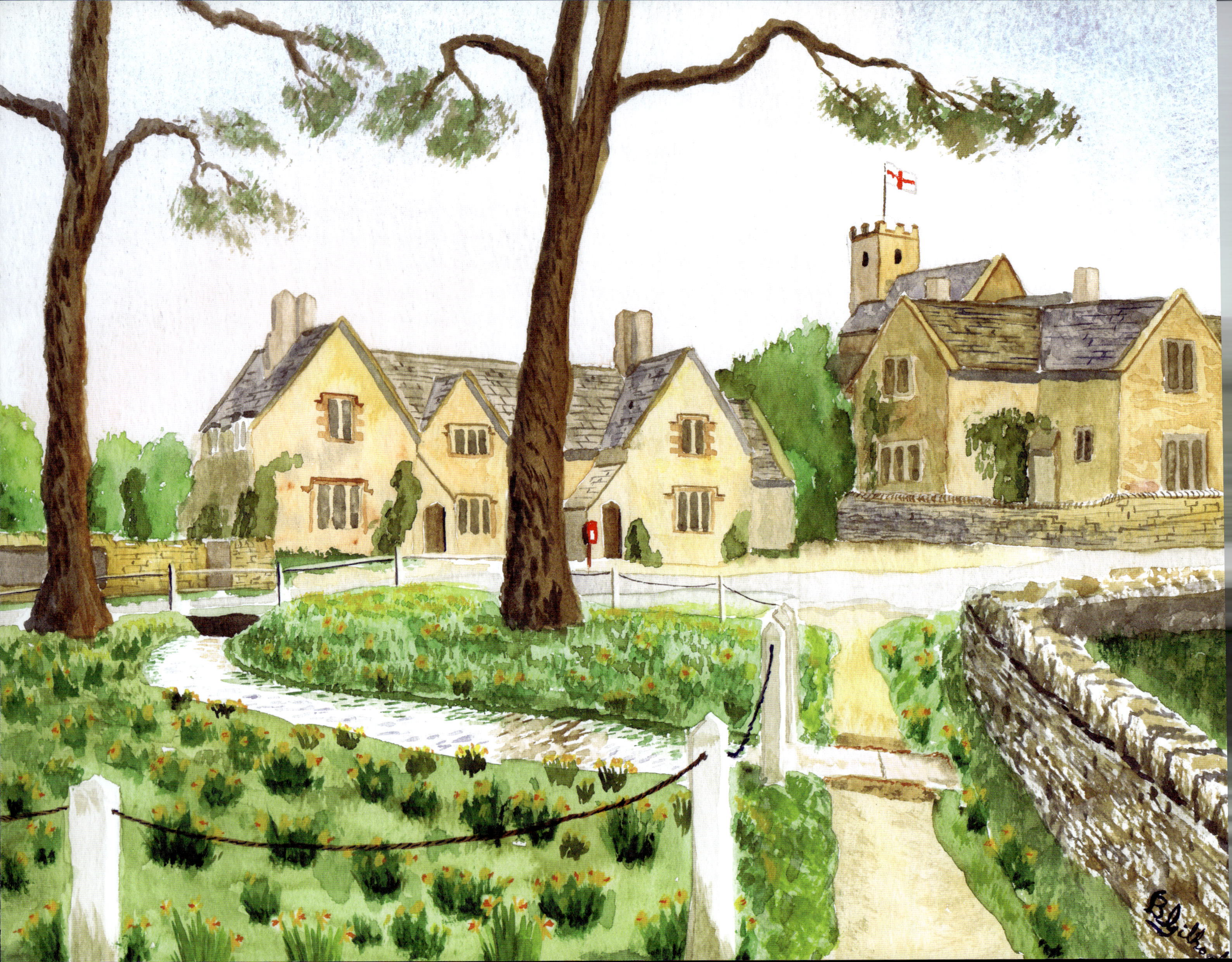

Minster Lovell

Still following the Windrush, Minster Lovell the village hides a sinister secret.
All centred around the splendid Manor House and the Lovell family.
The house was built in the 1400s .
In the latter half of the 1400 one of the descendants fought for King Richard 3rd at Bosworth Fields.
They were defeated and the young Lovell fled to Europe.
He returned, fought again, and again was defeated. Fleeing this time back to the manor house.
Once there, in fear of his life, he went into hiding.
Having a secret room constructed and once inside it was secured. (bricked up.)
Only a faithful servant bringing food and looking after Mr Lovell's needs knew of the rooms existence.
The servant died taking the secret of his master's whereabouts with him to the grave.
Unable to escape his self imposed incarceration, Lovell died there of starvation.
It was not until building work was carried out some 200 years later that the room was discovered
and the wretched skeleton found.
The last family to live in the Manor left in the mid 1700s. The house fell into disrepair and ruin.

We travel north again to Shipton under Wychwood

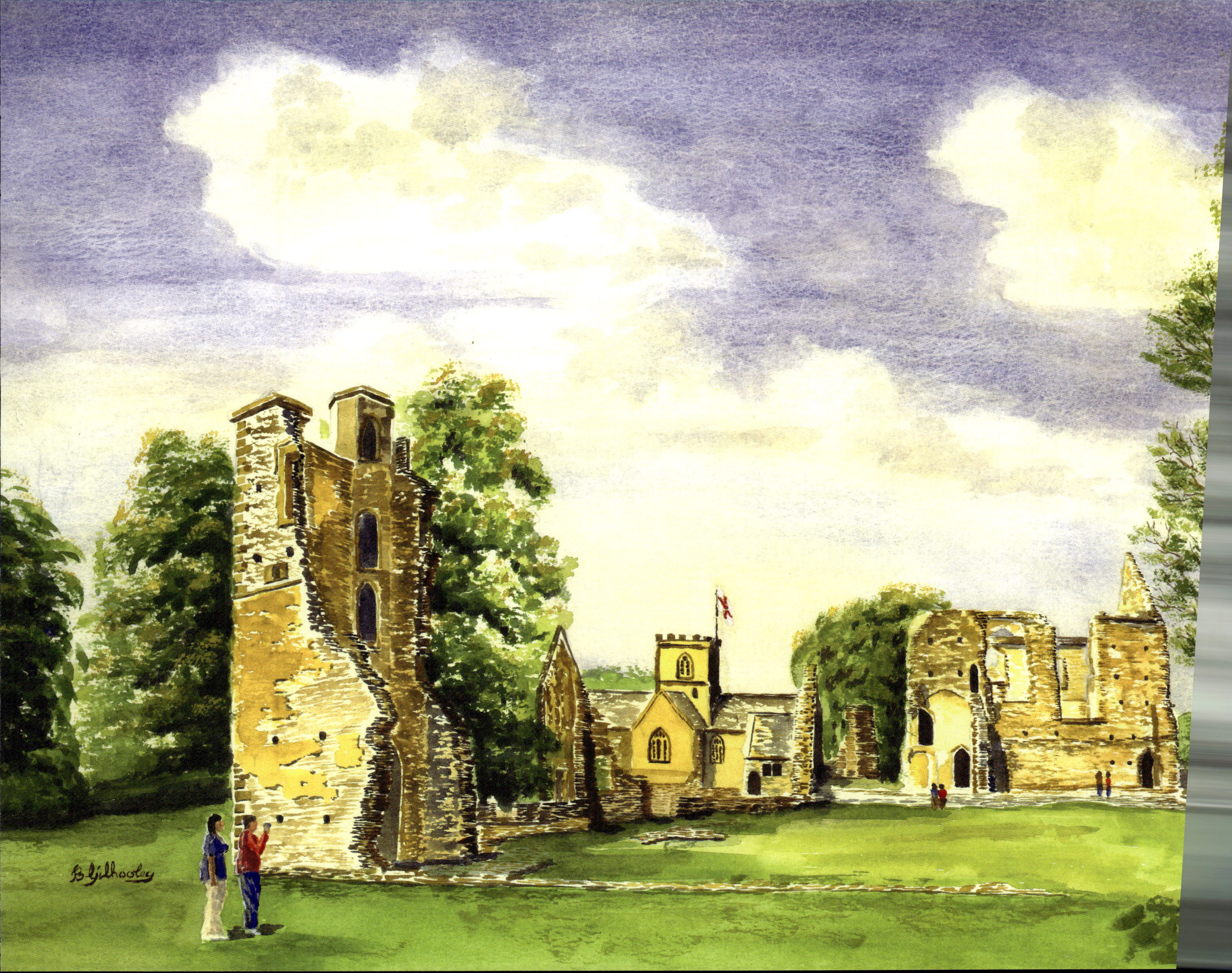
B Gilhooley

Shipton under Wychwood

Shipton straddling the busy A361. It is an interesting village and steeped in history.
Dating back to the Doomsday Book it had connections with the local abbey.
hence the prominent Shaven Crown Hotel on the main road. An impressive medieval
looking building with a striking doorway and mullioned windows.
Opposite is a wide green leading to the church in the distance. On the green stands a fountain and needle.
In memory of 17 parishioners who perished on a voyage in the Cospatric, in search of a better life in New Zealand
November 1874 the ship was destroyed by fire en route.
Further along the road is Shipton Court built in the 1600s. Fronted by impressive yew trees.
It is now private apartments. Opposite are wrought iron gates with a carriage drive beyond, lined by old Lime trees.
In the middle ages the area was heavily wooded and renowned for poaching and high way robbery.
Deer belonging to the crown finding their way to the lucrative markets in the city of Oxford no doubt.
Travellers today can enjoy the comforts of the hotel, or two other hostelries in the town.
Look out the Lamb Inn A comfortable Pub with B&B accommodation and delicious food.

Continue across country through the lanes north to Bledington.

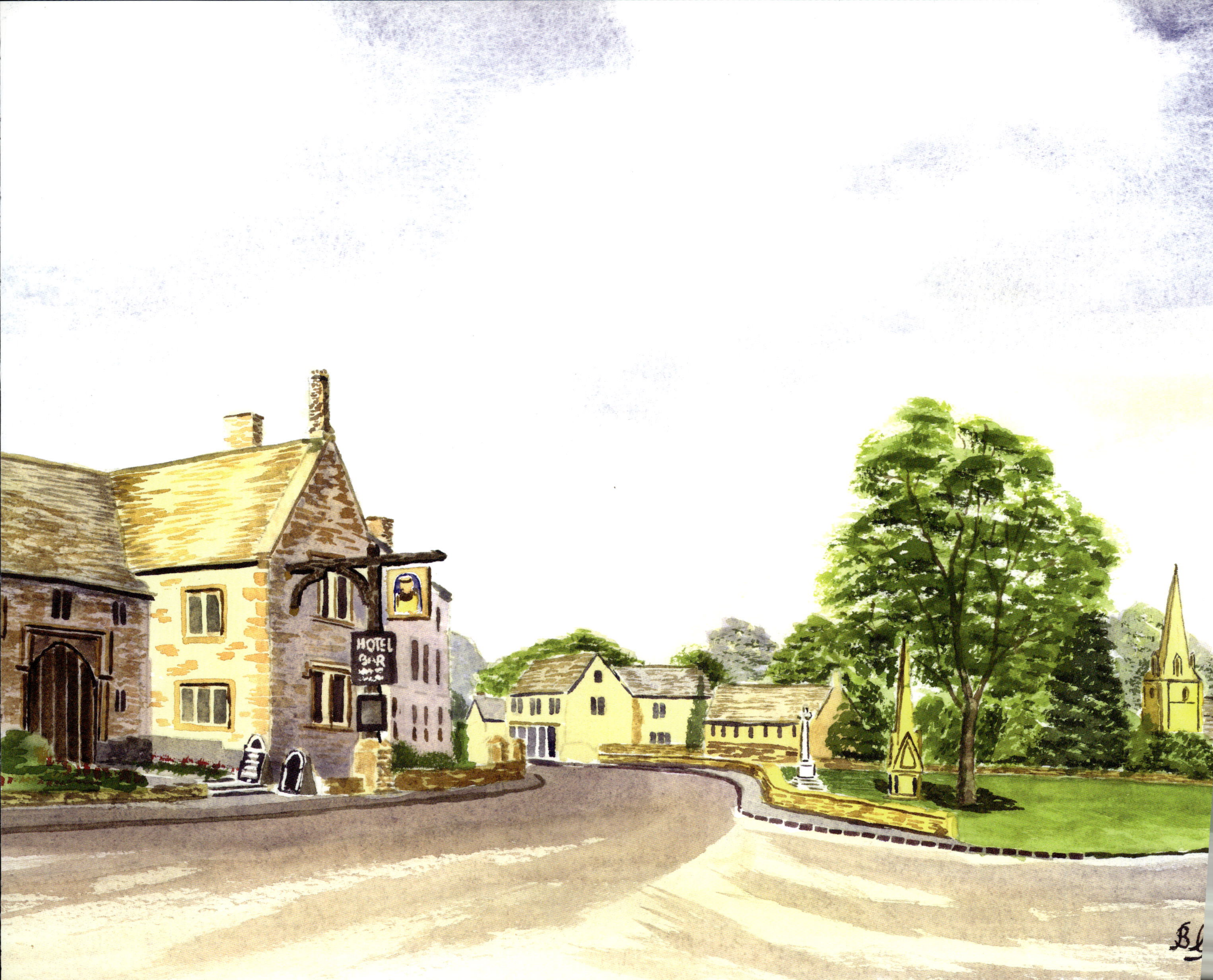
HOTEL

Bledington

On approaching Bledington signs warn you to slow your speed. and watch for Ducks.
The centre of the village has a very large Green with a stream running through it
This being very popular with local Mallards who wander freely having no care for motor vehicles.
The Kings Head comes highly recommended.
It has been known to have younger members of the present Royal family frequent its bar.
You can't get better recommendation than that. The food here is superb.
Parts of the church date back to the 12th centry.
The village was owned by the Abbey at Winchcombe in times gone by.
Some of the houses on the green have "up ended flag stone fencing." a feature in some
Cotswold villages.
For the ramblers amongst us The Oxford Way crosses close by with several other foot paths.

Now journey north to Stow on the Wold

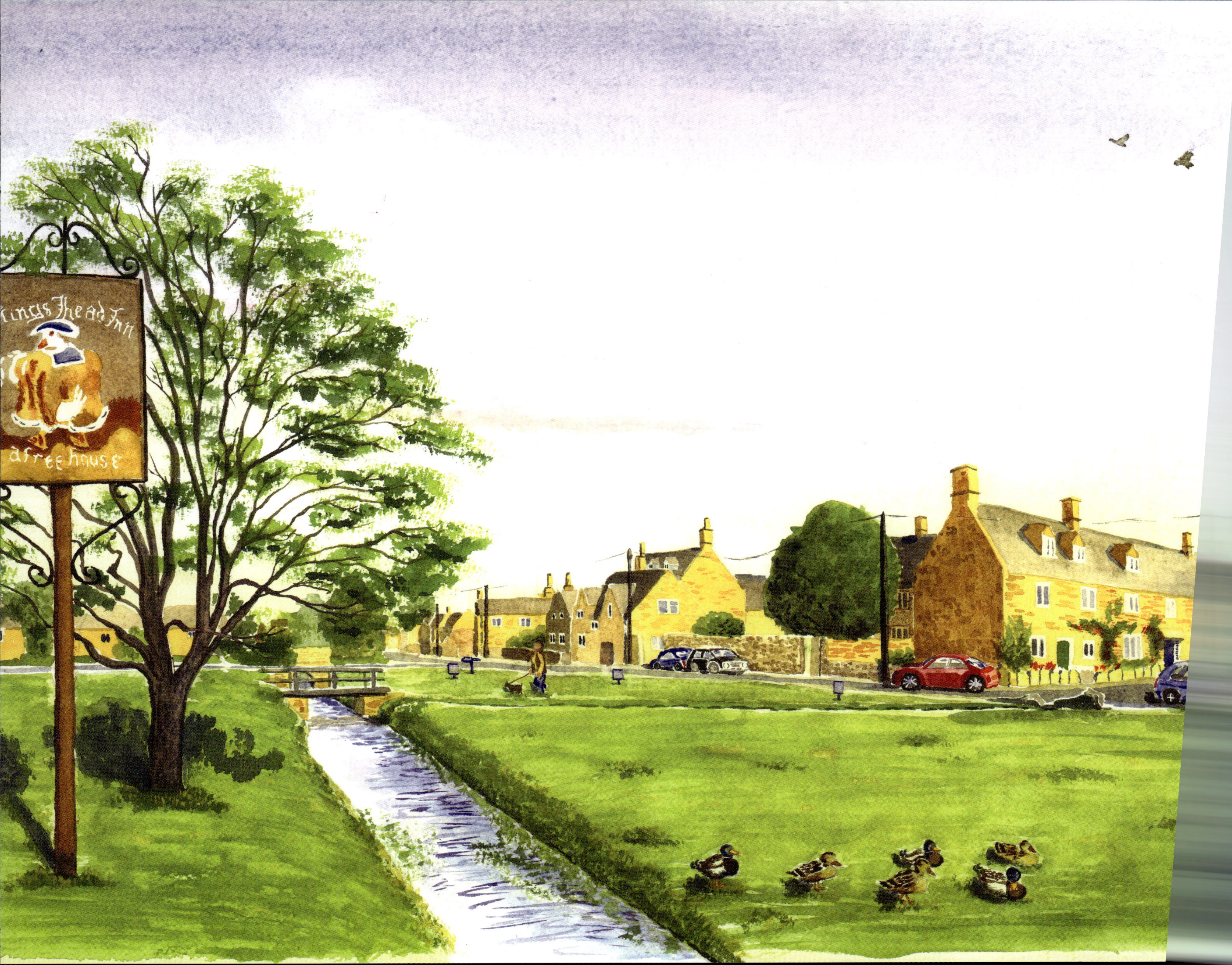
Head Inn
a free house

Stow- on- the- Wold

The high Wolds. Stow is the highest town in the north Cotswolds hence the rhyme
"Stow on the Wold where the wind blows cold."
With roads converging The Fosse North to South. Oxford through to Gloucester East to West.
Stow became an important market town. Even in the 1100s.
It was occupied by Oliver Cromwell in the Civil War and after several skirmishes some thousand royalist troops were incarcerated in and around the town.
The Church was even commandeered as a prison.
Today the town is renowned for the twice yearly famous Horse Fair .
When the travelling people with their horses, caravans and anything Romany turn up.
These days it is quite a good natured affair with families meeting up who perhaps haven't seen one another since the previous year. And the youngsters "Boys meet the Girls"
The rest of the year it is also popular with the day and coach trippers. The town has a reputation For quality antique shops and art galleries.
There is also a nationally known Kitchen and Garden retailer here.
Many old Coaching Inns in the Town all offering excellent accommodation and Good quality food.
The Royalist Hotel is reputed to be the oldest Inn in England.
On the north of the town, is a small green. Where stand the old stocks. Sit and try them out!.

Just outside Stow is Broadwell.

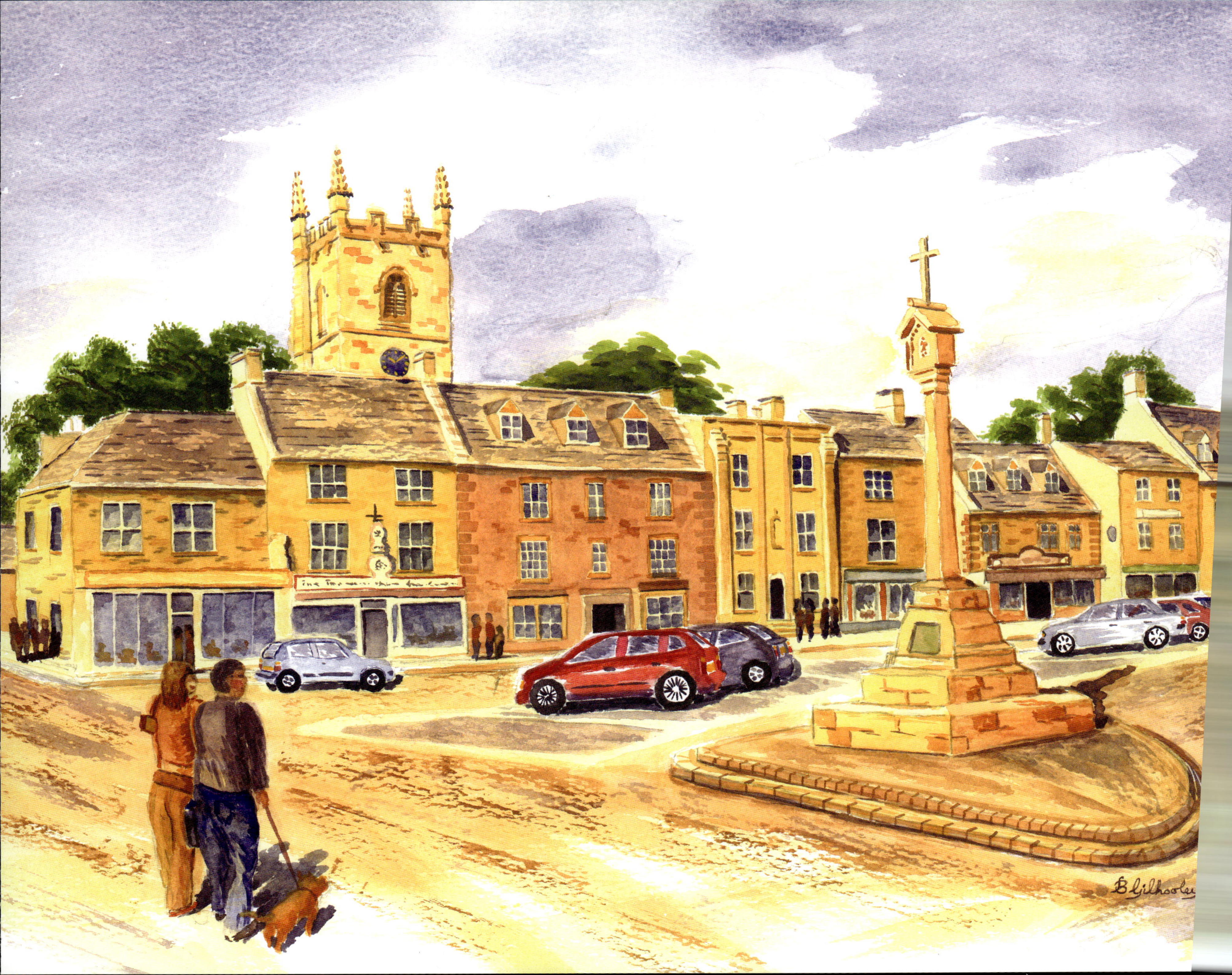

Broadwell

This is a charming and unspoiled village, golden stone houses cluster around a large green.
The green was presented to the villagers by Lord Ashton, for the grazing of their live stock.
He was once a resident of the village.
Alongside is a stream and to the far side washes over the road as a shallow ford.
Overlooking the green is the Fox Inn.
"Ideal for the grazing and watering of the human live stock."
The church further up the hill, is worth a stroll.
In the church yard there are tombs with unusual Wool Bale Lids.

Trekking eastwards we go to Long Compton and the ancient stones.

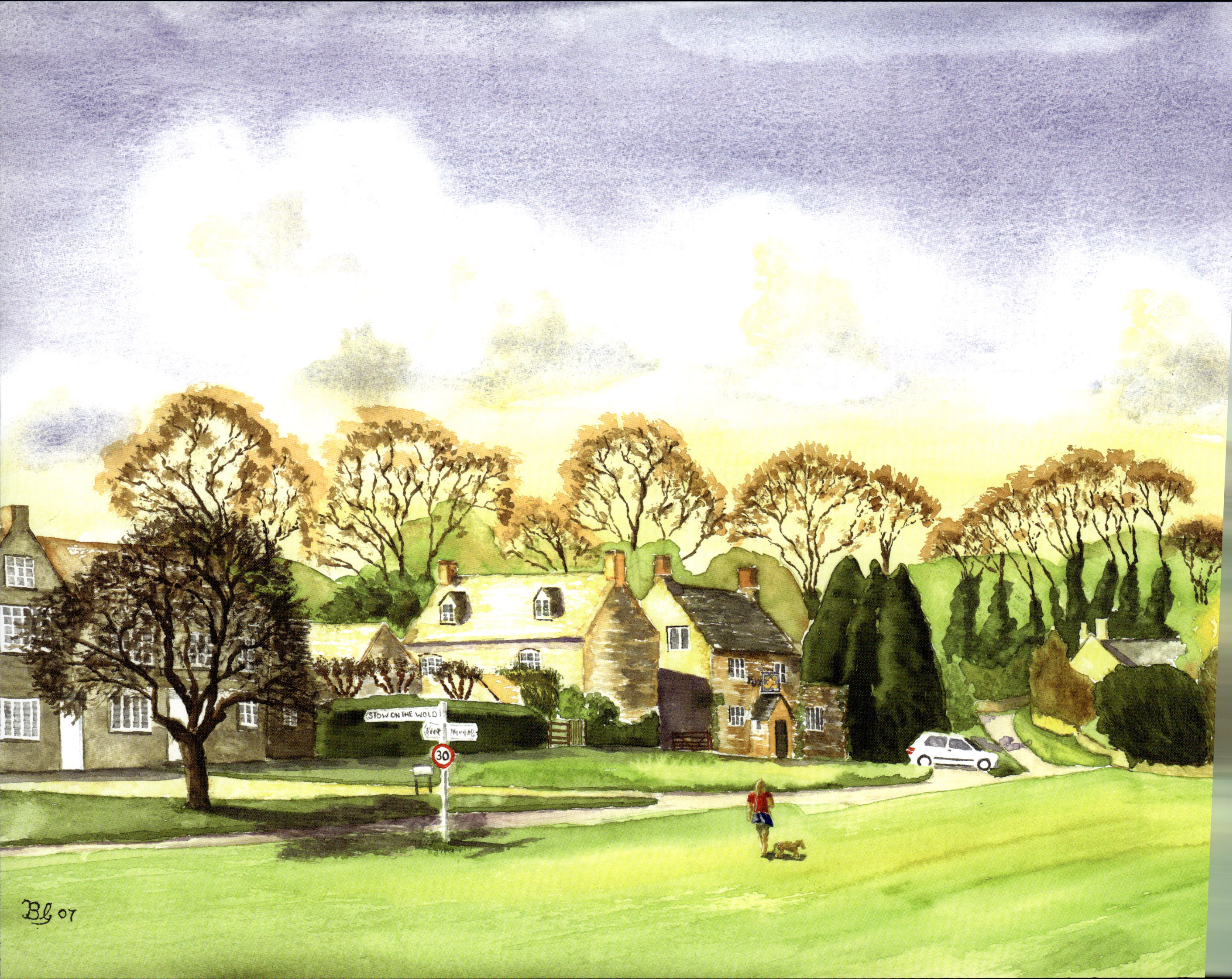
STOW ON THE WOLD
30

Long Compton

On the eastern edge of the Cotswolds, Long Compton can be found with its thatch cottages straddling either side of the busy A3400 road to Oxford .
Residents have a lot to put up with, with the heavy traffic rumbling through.
A point of Interest is the Church with its Lych-gate and a small committee room built above it.
Head towards Oxford and at the top of the hill to the left, a sign for Wyatt's Farm Shop invites you to Home made Ice Cream. Yum Yum.
This road leads you to a working farm with an interesting Garden Centre and extensively stocked Farm shop. A Butchery temps you with local meat produce.
And a relaxed Tea Room completes the experience.
Head back to the A3400 go straight over towards Little Rollright

On the left are The Rollright Stones.

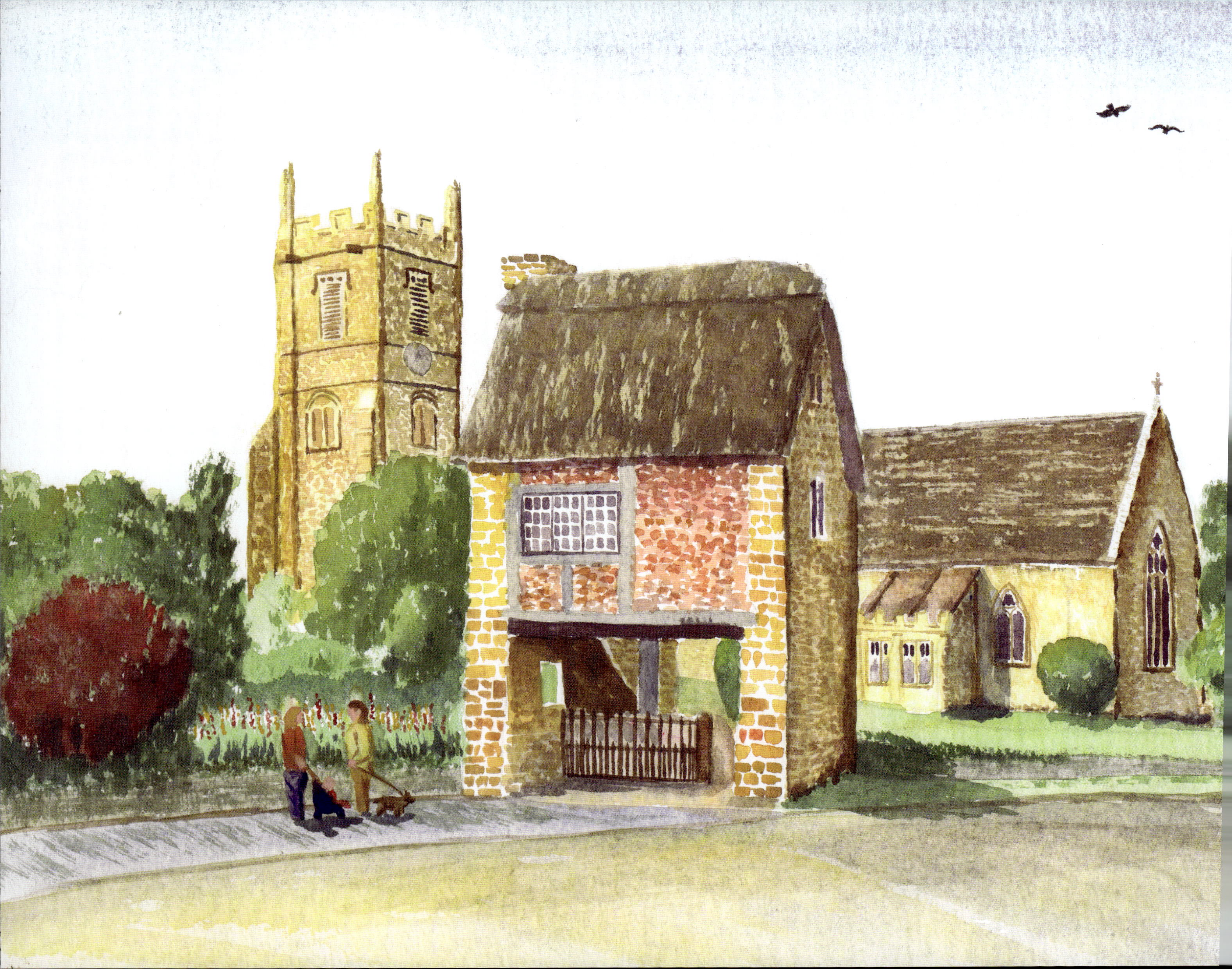

Rollright Stones

This is taking you right back to the Bronze Age.
Possibly 2500 years BC.
In a field one side of the road is the King Stone some 8 feet tall.
On the other side adjacent to the road is the Kings Men stone circle.
A little further along a foot path is the Whispering Knights.
There are some 65 to 70 stones in the circle but it is said you never get the same number each time you count them.
One theory is it was an early palisade wall with each stone touching apart from possibly one entrance. Or a hill fort.
Another is an encampment to keep out wild animals. Or possibly for religious ceremonies.
However they are all lost in the mists of time.

It is now time to come back to the 19th century and journey south to Chipping Norton.

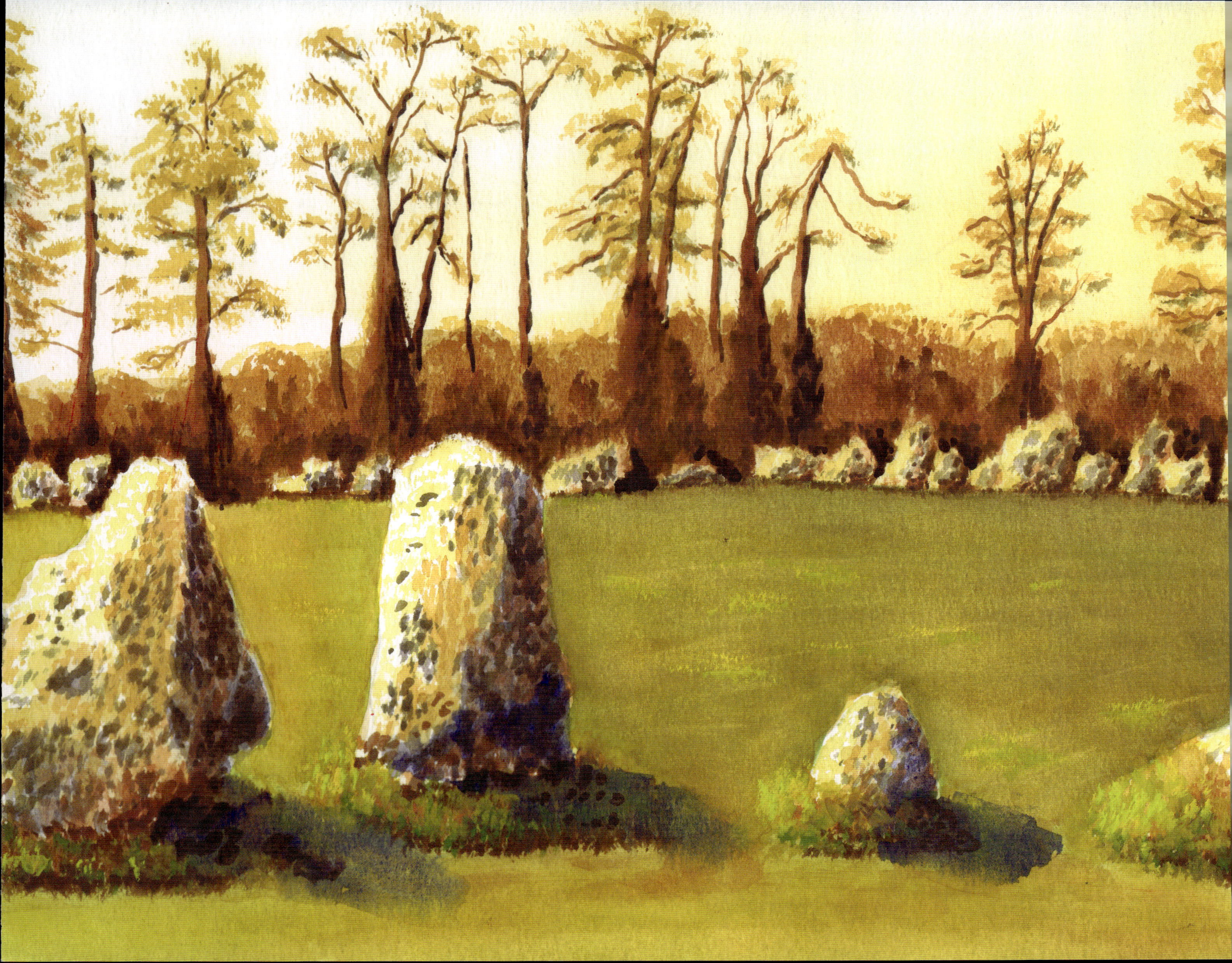

Chipping Norton

Chipping Norton is a bustling town sprawling down a hill side to the east of the Cotswolds.
Although not the most pretty it still has a charm of its own.
The most striking local building and most photographed by far is The Bliss Mill.
Though the town was famed for its wool market through the ages. It was not until the coming of the railway in the mid 1800s that this magnificent building came into being.
Rail was used to bring in coal to fire the steam engines. Smoke billowing from the huge central chimney and drifting along the valley on the still morning air must have been a haunting sight.
William Bliss the mill owner was making a fine quality Cotswold Tweed in the 19th century.
The mill is now converted to posh apartments.
The towns market is still held on a Wednesday.

A little closer to Oxford lies Woodstock and Blenheim Palace.

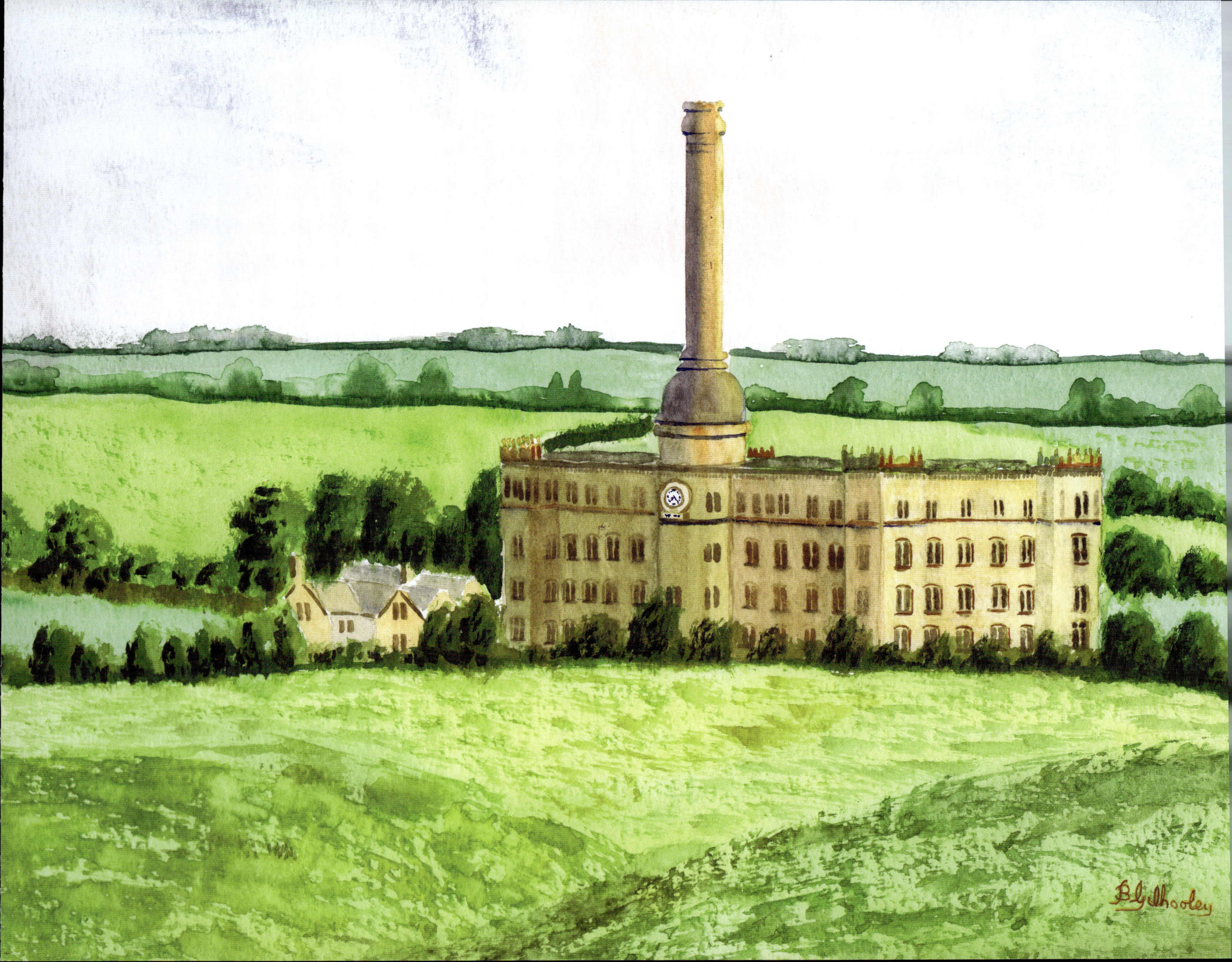
B Gilhooley

Woodstock

A busy little town it has tried hard to keep its Cotswold roots.
The main attraction a joining the town is Blenheim Palace
Seat of the Duke's of Marlborough and birth place of one of our greatest statesmen.
Sir Winston Churchill.
The village buildings retaining their beautiful stone facade.
Due to the popular tourist influx brought in by the Palace.
the interiors have been greatly changed to Cafes Restaurants and a variety of shops.
A farmers market is held regularly on a Saturday.
The Town hall also has frequent Art, Craft and Antique fairs on the weekends.
Numerous inns line the main street. The Bear being the most prominent and offering
High quality food

We now go to the centre of the blanket weaving towns. Witney

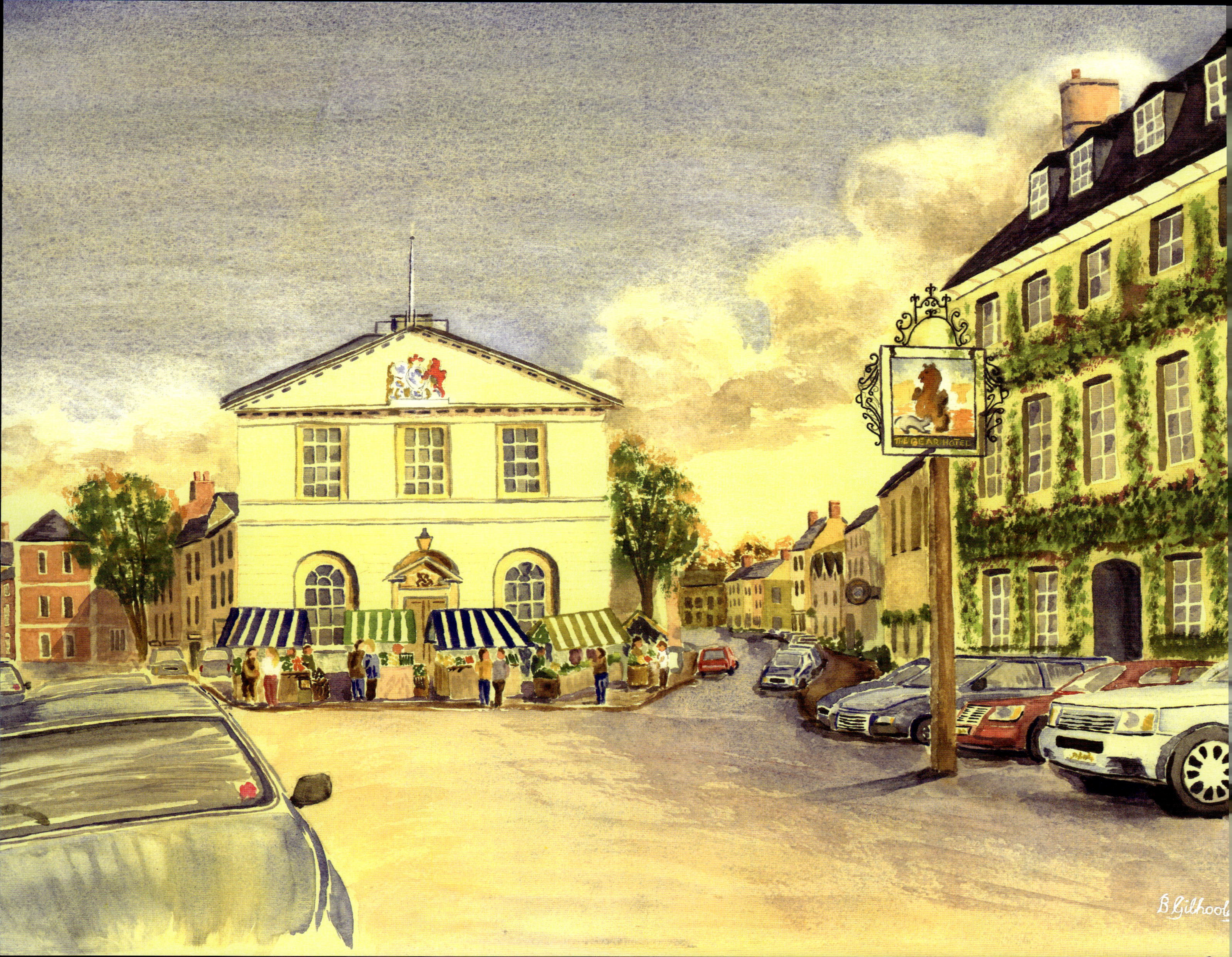
THE BEAR HOTEL

Witney

Although it is outside the designated area of outstanding natural beauty.
The town was famed for blankets made from Cotswold wool.
Due to the prosperity in the 17th and 18th century many elegant buildings arose.
making it the delightful town it is today.
The High Street. Market Place. leading on to a wide tree lined Green to the imposing
Spire of St Mary's church make a very fine town centre.
The Butter Cross a pillared. gabled roof market place with a clock turret above.
Built in 1683 so named due to the farmers wives selling eggs and butter in the dry
Whilst the cattle market took place a little way up. out in all weathers.
A weekly market is still held here every Thursday.
The Church Green is bordered by many beautiful golden stone buildings and historic inns.
The high street keeps its old buildings. With a sympathetic modern shopping mall
parking and supermarket bringing the centre of town into the 21st century.
The Blanket mills have now all closed dawn. "Earls" The world famed weavers of the 19th century
were the last to go. The mill redeveloped and now is residential apartments.

Travelling further south east we arrive at Letchlade.

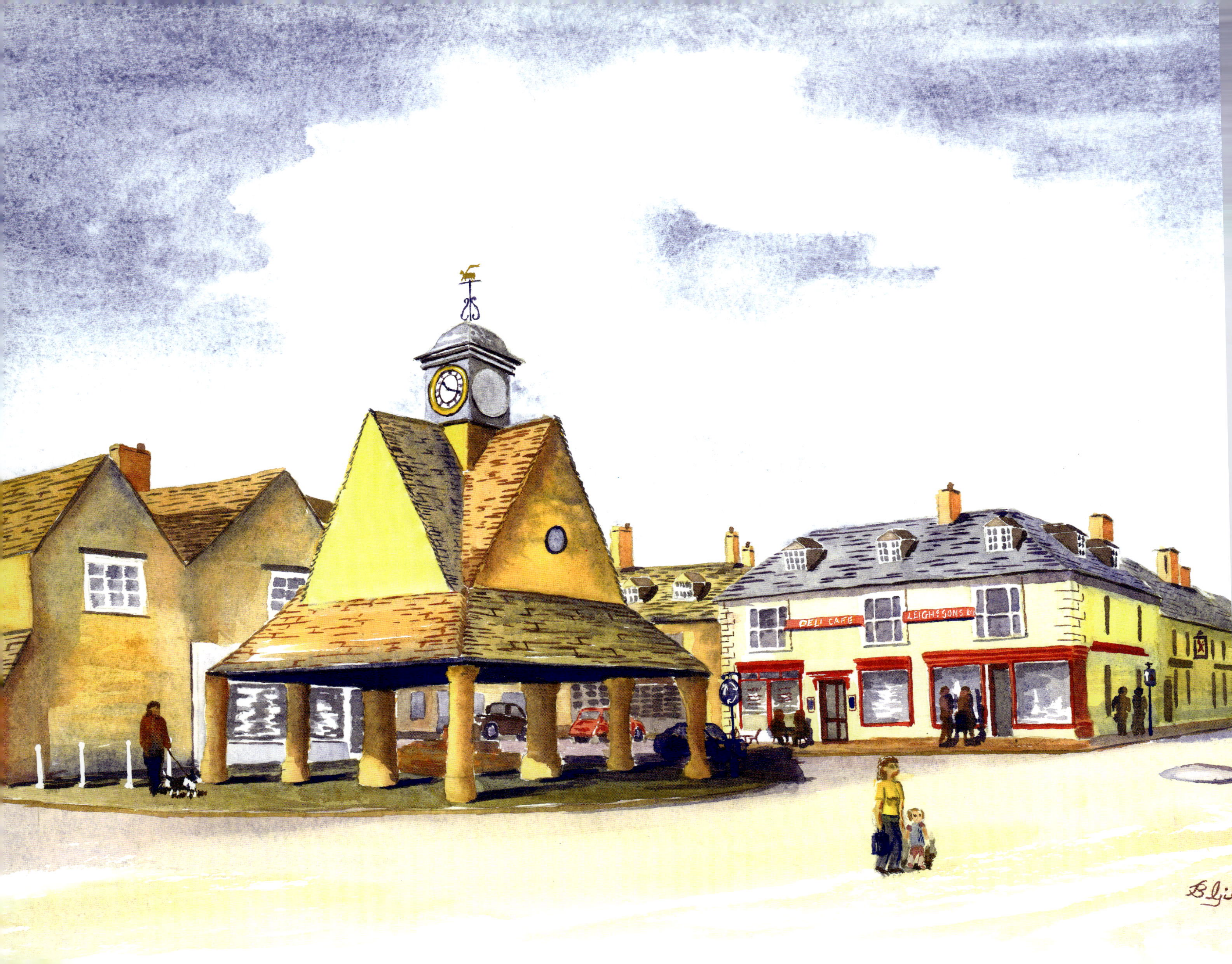
DELI CAFE
LEIGH & SONS Ltd

Lechlade

This is our first visit to the mighty river Thames. The river starts in the Cotswold hills in the fields just south of Cirencester. It crosses the Fosse way close to The Thames Head Inn.
(There is a foot path across the fields.)
As it reaches Lechlade it becomes navigable all the way to London.
This made Lechlade a very important inland port.
Goods from Wales in the form of coal and timber as well as live stock followed the Drovers Welsh Way.
Salt from Droitwich. Stone from the Cotswold quarries and Cotswold Cloth came down the Old Salt Way.
All this found its way onto barges at the quay side's in the town. Both prior to the Great Fire of London.
Then after, large quantities of quality stone was required to rebuild the capital city.
Although not as busy today, it is a pleasant thriving town. Popular still with river craft all be it the pleasure and tourist variety There are tranquil river side walks together with good quality hostelries to fortify the weary traveller.

Journeying south west we next visit the oldest borough in England.
Just off the A429 some 11 miles south of Cirencester is Malmesbury

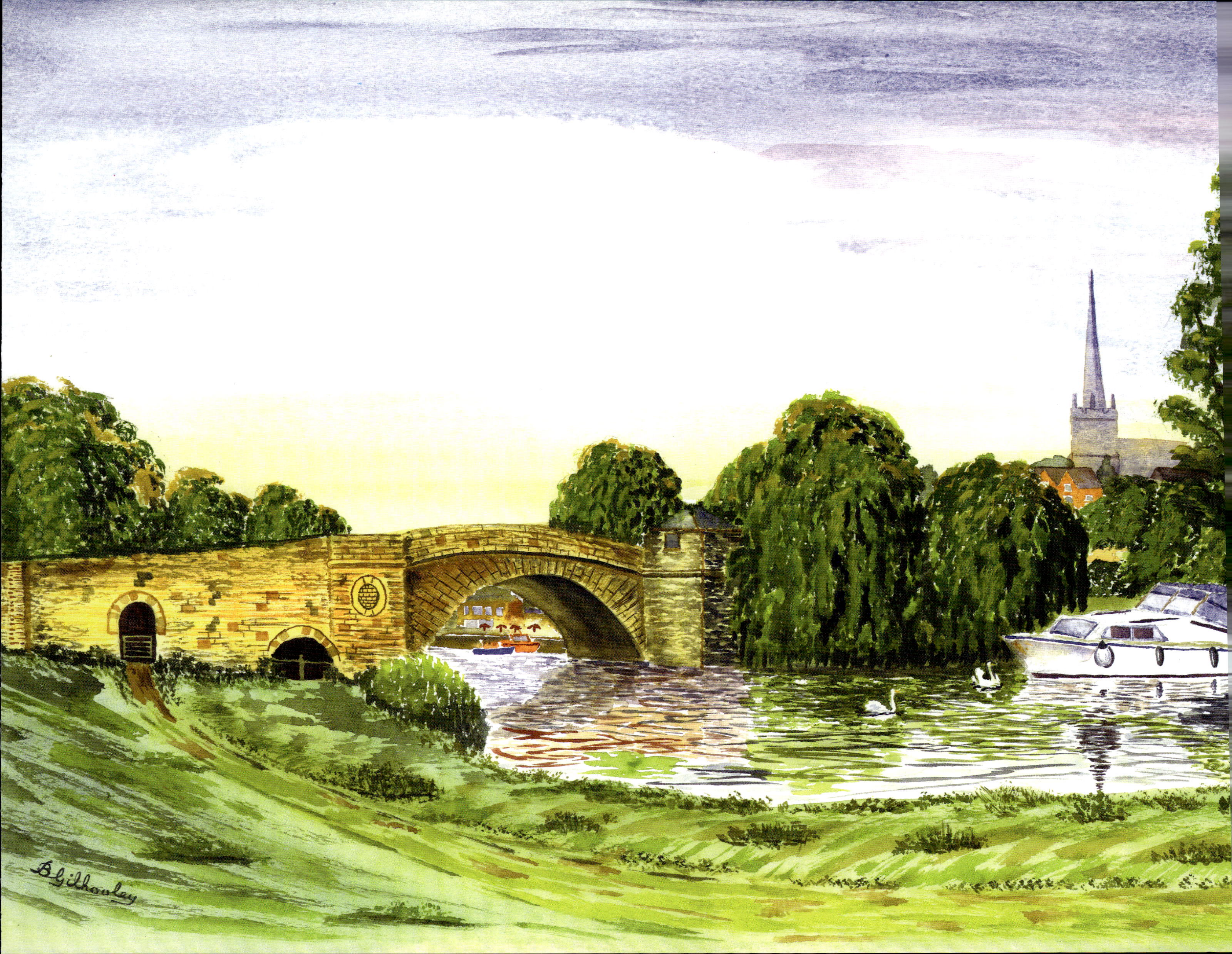
B Gilhooley

Malmesbury

Driving into Malmesbury and parking in the town square.
At first sight there does not seam much apart from the Town hall and Museum.
But wait! Go through the lane to the side of the town hall.
The old town and Abbey with the old Lantern top Market Cross opens out before you.
The market cross was built in the late 15th century. as legend has it.
" A place for poor folks to stand when the rain cometh."
It stands at the junction to the top of the high street and old market place. Close to the Abbey.
To the left is a path to the Abbey. A once splendid Benedictine Monastery dating from the 7th Century.
Housing the tomb of King Athelstan. Grandson of Alfred the Great.
In the 15th Century a disaster struck in that the spire. reputed taller than Salisbury Cathedral's
Came crashing down through the abbey.
Part of the Nave was rebuilt and still today takes services of worship.
The Entrance. through a huge and impressive carved Norman porch.
In the abbey grounds is a gravestone to a local girl mauled to death by an escaped tiger
from a travelling circus in 1703.
Go back to the market cross. Turn right by the Whole Hog inn. You will come to Cloisters Garden.
Here walk down to Abbey House Gardens. Home to the famed Naked Gardeners.
You are treated to 5 acres of beautiful formal garden walks. Some laid out as enclosed gardens rooms.
With Topiary shrubs and climbing roses.
By the restaurant is a pond garden with the biggest Koi I have ever seen.
Return back to the market cross and take a walk down the high street.

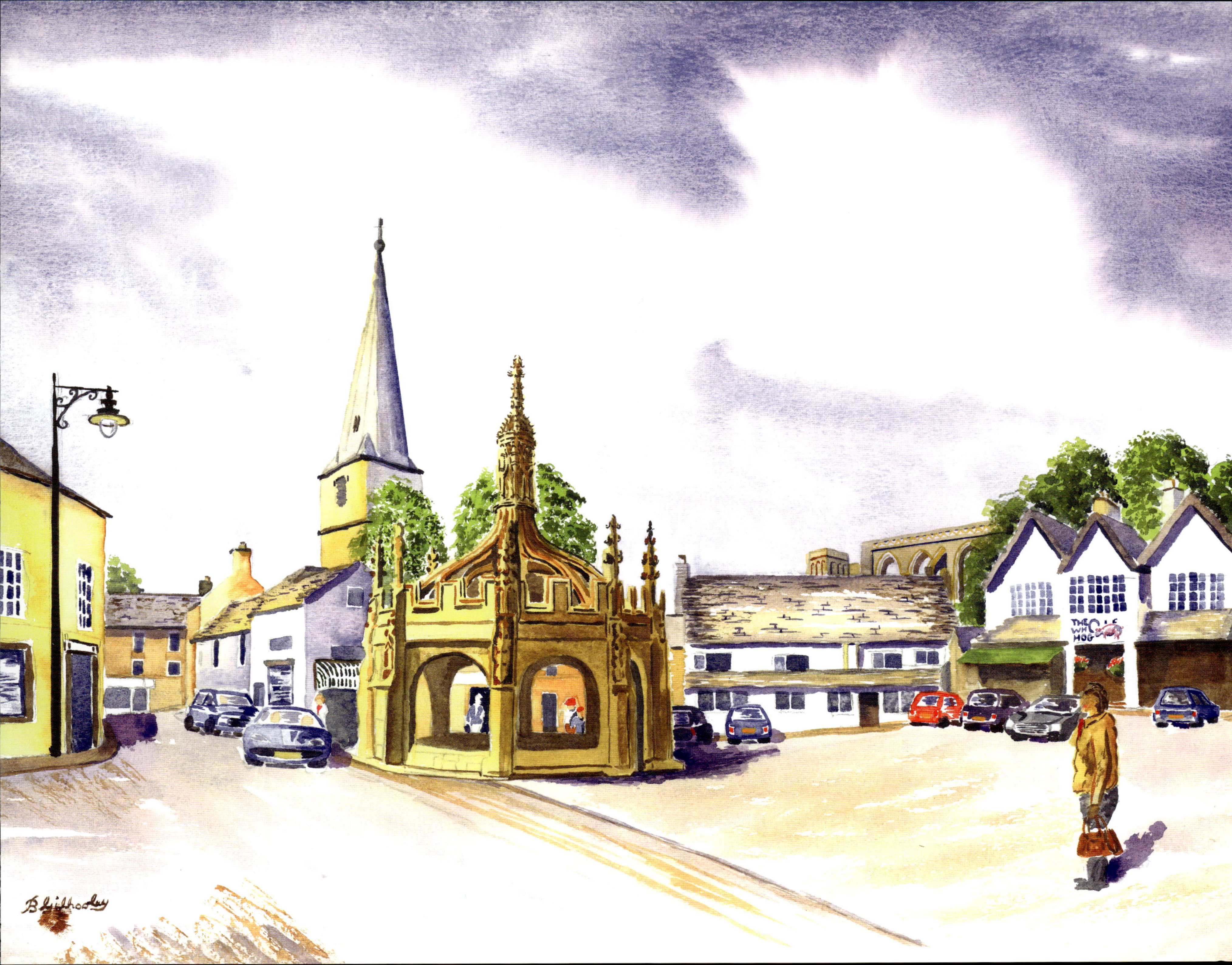

Castle Combe

Castle Combe is the most southerly village we visit on our Cotswolds journey.
Just 12 miles from Bath.
Park your car in the designated car park above the village and leisurely stroll down the hill.
As you enter the village you are treated to a row of individual and terraced houses all in the Beautiful golden Cotswold stone akin to Bourton, Stow and Morton.
In the market place you see a covered in market cross with a intricate carved central pillar
It dates from around the 14th century when the village was granted a Market charter.
The Castle was on the hill above the village. Alas it no longer exists. The site is on private land.
The village prospered like many Cotswold villages in the Middle Ages from weaving.
Mills were powered by the river at the south of the village. Now a pleasant babbling stream
The main street is a mish mash of weavers cottages and merchants houses.
Some stone, some half timbered, all with split stone roof tiles in the best Cotswold tradition.
It was the beauty of the village that led to the village being central to the film Dr Doolittle.
Two Inns in the village offer splendid tasty food and comfortable accommodation.

From here we head northwards again up to Tetbury.

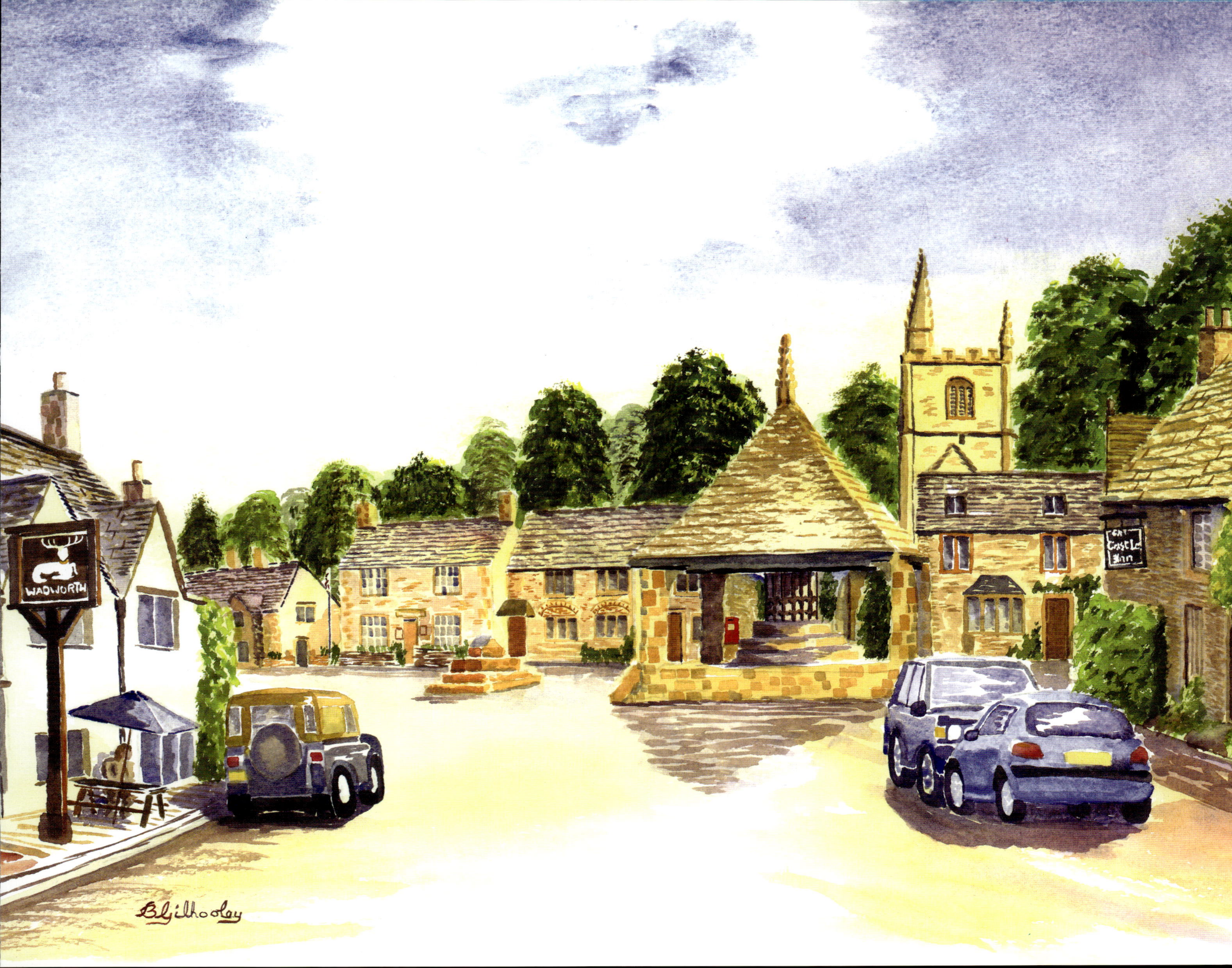
WADWORTH

Tetbury

There has been a settlement here from 680A D a monastery and fort resided here.
In the Middle Ages it again was a Cotswold wool town.
A tuscan pillared market hall with a Town hall above was built in the 17th century
The market still takes place every Wednesday and Saturday.
The town prospers today and is renowned for its high class antique shops
Some 25 in all.
Many shops have royal patronage due to Prince Charles and Highgrove close by.
Princess Ann is at Gatcombe Park and the Duke of Beaufort are all close at hand.
Tradition plays its part with the Wool Sack Race held every spring bank holiday Monday.
Men of the town race up Gumstool Hill with 48 Lb sacks on their back.. No doubt
the brave are fortified with local ale.

Ten miles further north is the old roman city of Corinium or Cirencester
In today's terms.

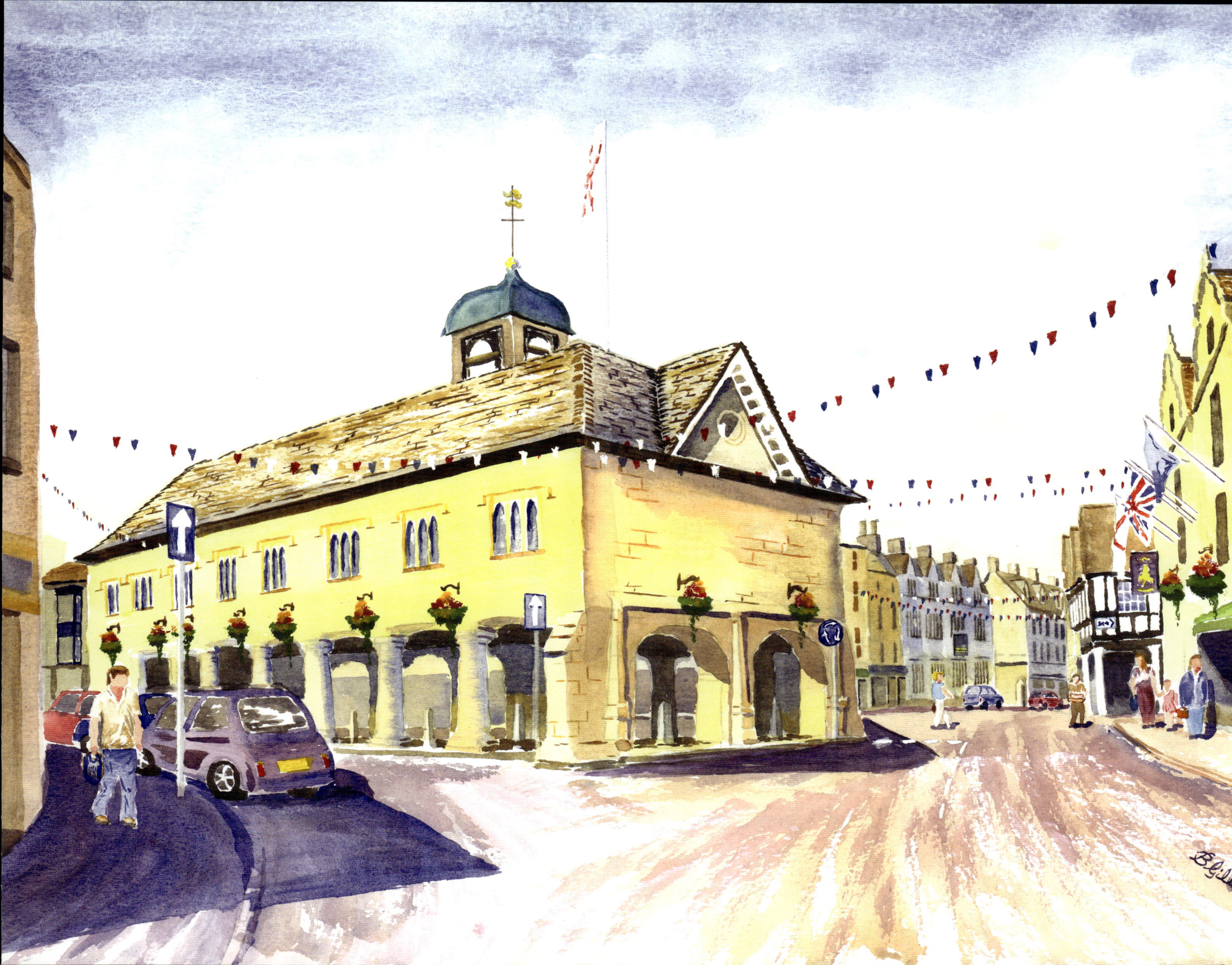

Cirencester

A cross roads for three major roman roads This held a large roman garrison and was the second largest
Town in Briton. Little roman evidence exists today apart from some stone walls and an impressive earth covered
Amphitheatre to the south of the town. Also the Corinium Roman Museum has collected a wealth of artefacts.
The Saxons paid little importance to the town. Favouring Winchcombe to the north.
It was not until the Normans and the industrious monks. In the Middle Ages. did the town prosper and grow once more. Later
wealthy wool merchants flourished here. They are responsible for most of the impressive old buildings
to be found in the town. See the wide market place with elegant shops together with the magnificent parish church.
Its lofty tower and ornate three storey porch. bear evidence to the towns wealth. The porch is a building in itself.
In the dissolution of the monasteries this building was taken over by the council and made the Town Hall.
Later it reverted back to the church.
The towns prosperity continues today with shops in the market place many. and most independently owned.
The old Corn hall has gone through a refurbishment and is occupied by small independent traders.
all doing good business.
A mansion and extensive park land lie on the west side of the town .The park land open to the public.
A polo club occupies part of the land. Here at times the Royals can be seen at play.
I recommend a booklet be purchase from the tourist office as there is lots to see locally.
I hope by just touching on a small part of the towns sights it has whetted your appetite.

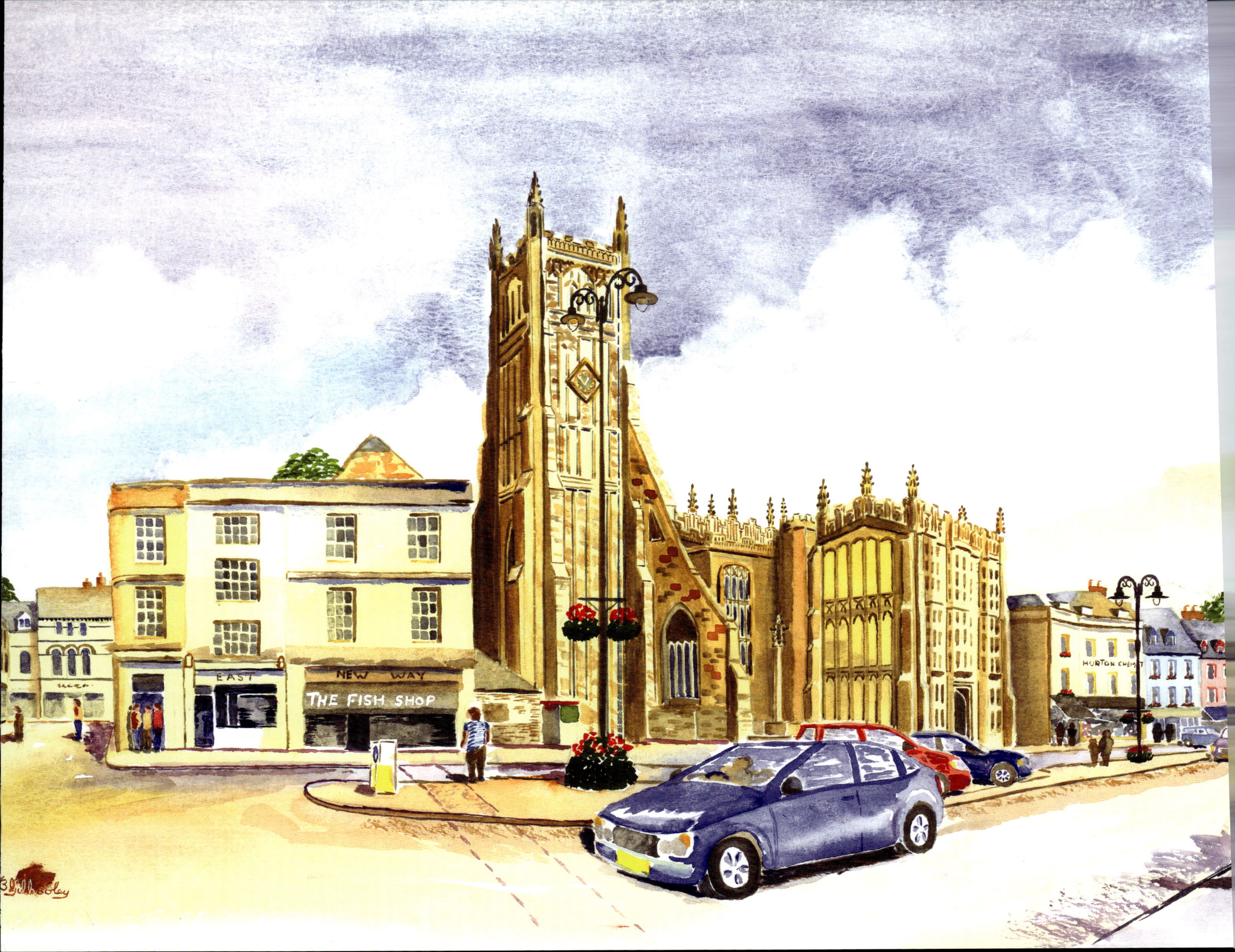
EAST
NEW WAY
THE FISH SHOP

Acknowledgements

I should like to take this opportunity to thank everyone who inspired me to compile this book.

Kit and Hazel for there input.
Ann Waller for her computer input.
Stan Kaminski Artist for his tutorage

Beverley my wife for her patience and encouragement whilst travelling around the area with me.
whilst I am painting the seines. "She is a long suffering painting widow'. I don't play Golf!"

And mainly your selves Dear Reader for taking time to read this book.

Alighting from your mode of transportation
And using your feet to enjoy this wonderful
countryside of ours.

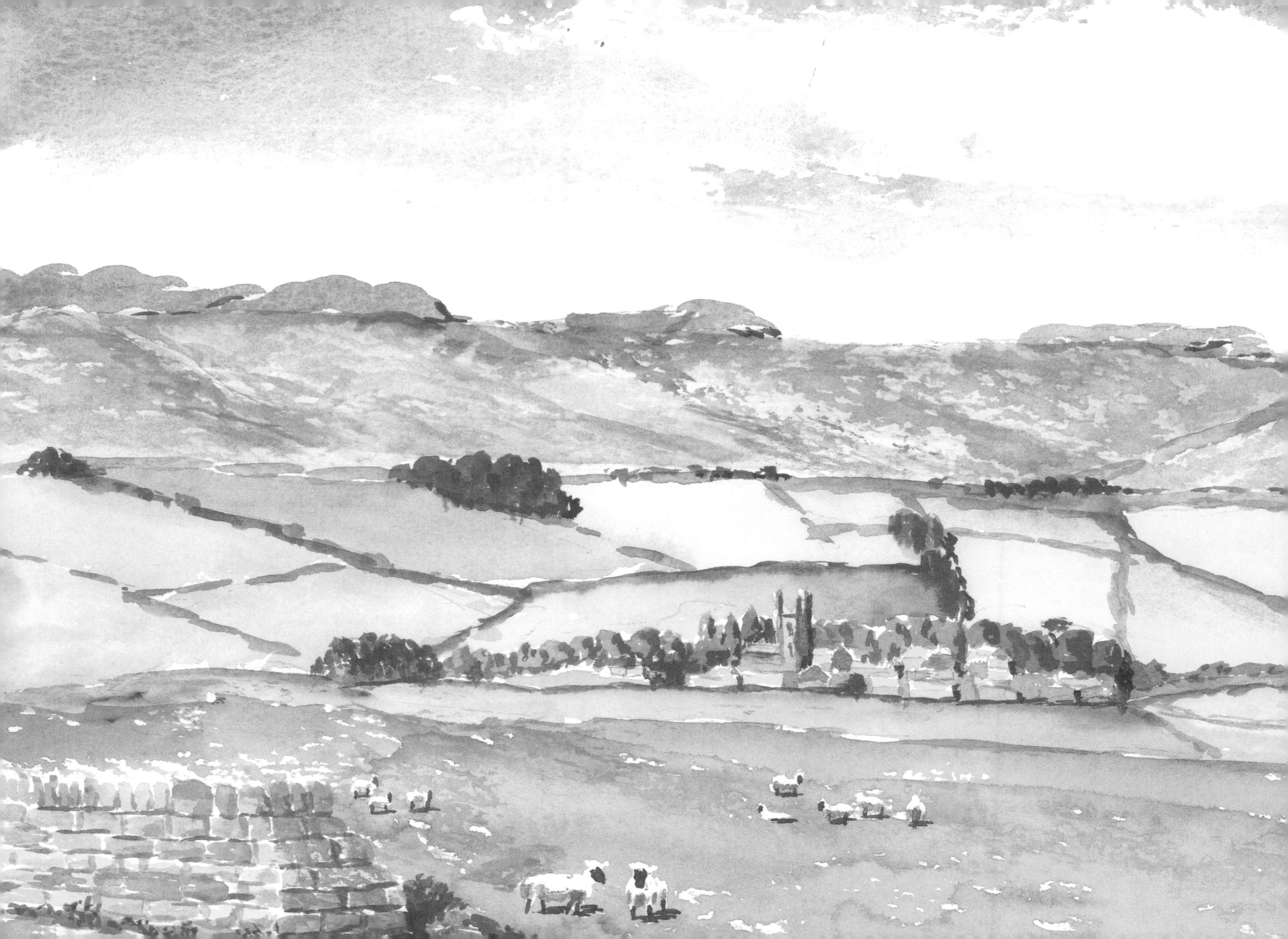